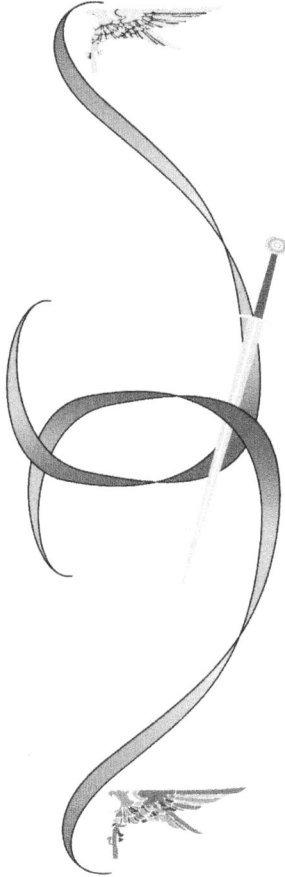

Going to the Center of God's Heart

© Copyright Sheri Hauser 2020
Published by Glorybound Publishing
Camp Verde, Arizona
SAN 256-4564
Printed in the United States of America
KDP ISBN 9798580570723
Copyright data is available on file.
3rd Edition
Hauser, Sheri, 1957-
      Going to the Center of God's Heart /Sheri Hauser
      Includes biographical reference.
1. Ancient Mysteries   2. Charismatic interest/Prophecy
I. Title

www.gloryboundpublishing.com

The cover image is used from Hubble NASA.

Books by Sheri Hauser

And Afterwards I will Pour Out My Spirit
Dream Language Understood
Faith on a Wing and a Prayer
Filled with the Holy Spirit
Going to the Center of God's Heart
Growing Ministry to Seed instead of Fruit
Intimate Relationship with Jesus
Living in the Haunted House of my Head
Living in the Shadow of the Sins of our Parents
Preparing the Bride of Christ: Allegorical
Sharing Prophetic Gifts in the Church
Simple Fun Christian Dream Interpretation
Spiritual Authority Over Demon Dragons
Tactical Demonic Warfare
Why the Glory Departed

Prophetic Prayer
Foundational Prophetic Prayer
Leading Prophetic Prayer
Manual of Personal Prophetic Prayer

Prophetic Arts
Christian Authors Driving the Market
Inspirational 3-D Poetry
Prophetic Interpretation of Art

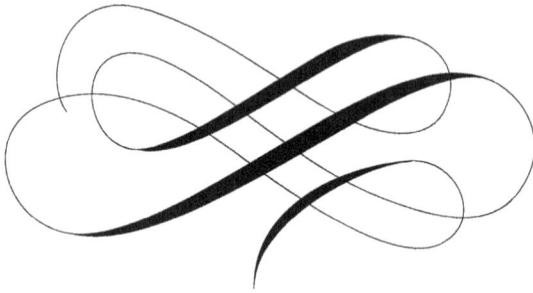

Going to the Center of God's Heart

Coriantá

By
Sheri Hauser

Glorybound Publishing
Camp Verde, Arizona
in the year 2020

I never started out to write a book, I just took the path that was laid out for me. This is a collection of writings that are compiled from dreams, visions, and revelations. They provide a matrix for the training that I have received from the Holy Spirit. The teaching is from topical Bible studies. I have spent hours and hours hiking in the desert outside of Las Vegas.

The sayings that I label 'words' are given to me by God asleep, as well as when I am awake. Some of them are dreams that have 'subtitles'. Others, stand alone without a dream.

The book is a picture book. It is word pictures. It takes the hard issues of the Kingdom of God and presents them as pictures. They were given to me in pictures, and I present them to you the way they arrived.

There is an empty book on my night stand that He fills day and night. To me, the dreams are like gold threads coming down from heaven containing the voice of God. I try to catch as many as I can. I have accepted every dream as being a word from God and treat each with honor bringing them all back to Him for help to understand them.

I asked Him once, "Why do you bring me these dreams like riddles? I have to work so hard to get them open."

He answered me, "Dreams are like boxes under the Christmas tree. Each one is a present from Me. Does a Father put all of the Christmas presents under the tree unwrapped? No, he wants to see the face light up when the gift is opened. I want to share the delight."

The start of it all happened when He gave me the same dream over and over. In this dream I have a set of keys in my pocket that have been left by my father. In the dream, he has doesn't need them, he left them for me. Since I have memorized a lot of Scripture, I knew some verses on keys. God called them to my mind. I took this information to a special friend who I knew was close to God. Over some fried chicken, I asked him if it was possible that God could be talking to me in this dream. He was quick to affirm that God had talked to a lot of other people in the Bible, why couldn't He talk to me? So, I embarked on a study of the keys. I came across the most amazing verses in Revelation which indicate that Jesus left us the keys to the Kingdom of God when He went to heaven. So, I asked God to tell me the answer. Over the next three months, He gave me a dream, about once a month.

Each of those dream brought me back to the same section of scripture. After that I would be quick to write down any dreams and look over my Bible to see if the topic was in there. Because I don't turn the light on when I write the dreams in the night, they were messy.

In the morning, I would type them into the computer. So, I developed a dream file. It was for me. I never knew that others could do it. I typed interpretations of dreams for two years before I had a dream that told me God wanted me to write a book. I was shocked. I had never written anything before, except in school. So, I was terrified at knowing how to put the book together. I decided to put it together three times, so I could be sure how it went. So I started out compiling the dreams into some sort of files. After I spent a year putting the book together twice, I decided to fast. The third time I put it together, I fasted 40 days from bread and meat. I lost 20 pounds, and the dreams jumped to a new level. Whereas I had been having the picture type of dreams, I now began having word dreams. They came like ticker tape messages in the night. During the fast, I remember, one night, I became frustrated, because I was having little dreams. I would have a clip of about 10 minutes, wake up, write it down, then try to drift off to sleep. So, after an hour of this, I got up and sat in a chair downstairs. I figured that if I was quiet and stayed in the dark, I could continue to snooze and the words would continue to come to me.

They did. I stayed in that chair for several hours in the middle of the night. In the morning, when I typed the dreams into the computer, I had 9 typewritten pages. So, I pressed God. I continued to fast another 20 days. During this time, the nighttime word dreams were pushed over into the day. Now, if I focus on listening to God's voice, His words will come to me. One of the most profound writings on Angels was written in the middle of a church service. The message that I have been given is that God wants to speak to everyone. He wants to have an open path of communication with all of His children. These words were given to me. But, because He told me to, I now share them with you because He told me that if I share them with you, you will reach out for Him… and He wants you to. I am a one topic person. I pray. And, I pray for you, as you read these writings, they will enrich your soul and encourage you to seek Him in a new way.

God Bless, Sheri

Mine

Speak to my heart.
The heart will speak to the child in me.
Then I will understand.
I sought heaven and He met me on earth.
Be still and know that I Am God.
When you are still, and you let Me talk to you.
All will know Who I Am.
I own the quietness when I own you.
It's mine as you are Mine.
Let's be Mine.

Chapters

Carry His Heart

Be the one in a million who will carry his heart on a necklace on the outside of your shirt.

His heart over yours like his face over yours.

Be the one millionth caller to win the free trips to Heaven's throne daily.

Open our eyes and look to the fields.

They are white for the harvest. It's not snow, it's little flowers. Little dancing flowers. Smell. Amazing grace.

Even I notice. You hold the flowers that you didn't grow. You only hold. I grew by My hand. They are cut but they continue to grow. Colors on paper run when heated. Get the iron, get the wax paper. Heat and press. Beautiful colors running together to form a picture that wasn't planned by you. Press it.

Pressed flowers. Spring flowers. Delicate between the layers of pages. Behold the love! Look.

He's on the pages! Fragrance and love together mixed and pressed. Turn it over. Page by page. Smell Him.

Chapter I

Jesus is Alive

The rescue of God breaks through. His brokenness breaks through our brokenness in a place that only exists in the mind of God. That is called faith.

Window of Opportunity for Salvation

The Dream:
He got sick and died. He was my brother in law. I dreamed that he lived. He starts to move and we watch. Then he comes back to life and is grabbing at me, chasing me around. He is sick and has a green puddle coming out from his body. There is a surgeon who says he needs to have his gall bladder out. You can see it's needed. The surgeon tells him that he needs the surgery, then he must die. He has to go back to being dead. The brother in law cries and does not want to stay dead.

I realize that the reason he came back to life is that he is not saved. There is a lot of noise. I scream over the noise to tell him how to be saved.

There is a woman in front of his face, but she freezes and is unable to explain to him how to be saved. She can't talk because she is not ready. It is a Christian friend who wants to learn how to become closer to God. The television is too loud and there are too many people there.

To me it is simple to lead a man to Christ. But, to others, they have never done it. All I did was to ask God why he would bring him back to life, to have him die again. And, God responded that the man had been given a window of opportunity for some reason. It had to be salvation.

To us the dead guy is still dead, even though he does not feel the same way. Surgery, at this point is therapeutic, not meant to heal him. He is dead. We consider him dead. Then, I realize it is a spiritual condition, not a physical one. He looked dead to me, even though he is talking and following me around. Because, the truth is that, until he is made alive spiritually, he remains dead. We don't think it is that bad being dead, because we are alive. But, he seems to.

Interpretation:

There are those who follow the law, rather than the love of God. The law was never meant to save, it merely shows us our sin, so that we will see our need to be saved. Those who know about God's rules, yet never come to know Him personally, are dead, even while they walk. They are sick, in need of a physician, yet they do not seek one because they do not think they need one. It is much easier to convince a poor convict that he needs Jesus, than a successful Church going individual. The poor convict knows that he is a sinner in need of a Savior, but the other man may not be so keenly aware of his need.

There are those who are near me that are really dead, even though I think they are alive. We do not know one another's heart. Those who are not alive through Salvation in Jesus, are like walking dead people. Their spirit is dead, but their body is alive. They die twice because there is a physical death and a spiritual death.

In my dream, I dream that the brother in law is alive and he starts to move. I envision life for him, and it begins to happen. As I pray for him, the gift of life is extended to him. He is grabbing at me because he knows that I have something to offer him. I know how to offer him what he needs to live eternally.

He needs his gall bladder out. The gall bladder makes it so that we can absorb fats into our system. The Holy Spirit is oil. This man needs the oil of the Holy Spirit to be absorbed into his system. He has the inability to absorb it. He was never saved, so he was unable to absorb the things of God. We cannot have the Holy Spirit without salvation through the blood of Jesus. The surgeon will remove the capacity for him to know the Holy Spirit. Then, at that point he will truly be dead.

The man cries out for help, but others are very busy with their own schedules. They are distracted with watching television. Remember, I pray because I see a dream. A dream is a vision, just like television. Instead of allowing the world to give me their visions, I rely on God to give me His. And, God's vision for this man is to save him from eternal damnation.

A problem with this man getting saved is that the woman who is put in front of him doesn't know what to do. Why doesn't she know what to say?

What is obvious to me is only obvious because I ask God for the answer. But, when I ask Him, He makes it plain to me what the problem is. I believe the window of opportunity is for the woman as much as the man. God has given her an opportunity to be used within his kingdom, yet she is not ready.

It takes more than just being available, to be ready to respond when God asks us to. We need to study the Bible and learn what it says. Then, we need to learn how to ask God questions and wait for His responses. As He gives the responses, we need to be willing to follow His leading. It was noisy in the environment that He placed me in, I ~ But heard His voice because He dropped His message into my spirit.

The man had a dead spirit that could only be made alive through regeneration through the invitation of the Holy Spirit into his life.

If you know within your heart that you are dead, and don't want to stay dead, here is a prayer that you can pray to have assurance that you will live forever:

> *Father,*
>
> *I want to accept Jesus Christ as my Savior. I know that I am a sinner in need of a Salvation. I don't want to have my gall bladder out, but I want the Holy Spirit to enter into my body. Make my body to become the temple of the Holy Spirit. Please forgive me of my sin through the blood of Jesus Christ and give me eternal life. I renounce Satan and all of the world's ideas. Please teach me to love You... Amen.*

Do not fear what they fear; do not be frightened. But in your hearts set apart Christ as Lord. Always be ready to give an answer for the hope that you have. But do this with gentleness and respect. Romans 5-8, I Peter 3.15

Two Ships

It is like He has sent two ships to rescue His people.

He came to bring a ship that is like an aircraft carrier.

It has all the provisions necessary to feed, clothe, wash, and arm us. There is another ship coming toward us on the horizon.

It is His return we look for His promises to become the provision; For, the future to come to us.

We stand in the center, looking for Him to meet us from both directions. The past and the future, crashing into our now.

We can rely on His promises from the past, the Holy Scriptures, and for the future.

They meet now. A crash of power, like two waves of current coming together. The river of His knowledge meets the Sea of His love and grace. The river of mercy meets the sea of kindness.

The Holy Spirit sent through Jesus comes into us and meets both the river and the sea. The past and the future. The promise meets the hope. Faith meets provision through prayer.

That is exactly where I want to stand. *Father, place us in the place where we see the promises, pray them in, and look for Your provision. May our faith in Your promises meet Hope, through Your power. May Your waves clash in our lives. Bring our Hope to shore.*

The Bridge of God

It is like the Father went to deliver the mail to us and the bridge was out over the river. He sent His Son ahead of Him to repair the bridge. There was a terrible battle with a Sea Monster. He won the battle, only to reach the other side and be killed by the natives He was to bring the message to. They saw Him and were frightened because He didn't look familiar to them. He was a stranger. He died, but the bridge that He had spent 33 years building stood strong as ever. It had mighty girders that went to the bedrock and strong timbers that stand the test of time. This bridge lasts forever. So the Father came across the bridge. He must step over the blood splatters of His Son. First, He picked up His Son and brought Him back home with Him. But, then, instead of blowing that bridge up, He used it to walk back to those people that killed His Son when He had brought the first message. Because of His great love, He continues to cross that bridge by the Holy Spirit that is still splattered with His Son's blood in an attempt to deliver messages to us. It isn't a perfect system because our reception isn't good and, often, we don't understand His language. But, if we concentrate on the message we can get it.

Kabod

Long ago God spoke to people using the prophets as mouth pieces to deliver His message. But, now He has sent us a human message.

He didn't speak through Jesus Christ, but was in Him. God made the world through the arm of Jesus, He spoke through the prophets for a while.

That is the difference between prophets and Jesus? The Lord appointed an heir, Jesus. He is the radiance of God's Glory. He is the outflow of God's light and power. He is the heat in the air. The warmth of His Father flows from Him. He is the 'kabod'; the heaviness, worthiness, awesomeness of God.

He is the intrinsic worth of God's being.

Jesus is the Absolute, Perfect, Holy, Revelation of God.

God, Outside the Church

Our focus is not self sacrifice, but His.
Not temporal issues, but eternal.
Spiritual answers are found outside the Church.
God is bigger than that.
For, He made the earth and all that is within it.

Jesus as a Prophet

Is Jesus a prophet or God? Both. For, He was sent with a message. The message was not a note from God, however. It is the difference between sending a letter and mailing yourself. Jesus was God, mailing Himself to us. For, He was the very form of God, the Father, packaged in a body, just like ours, so that we might understand Him and learn about His love. The prophets all have messages of God's love, as well. But, many times, they also carry messages of other things. They might speak of direction, sin, and encouragement. And, certainly, Jesus came with powerful words from God delivering messages from Him of the need for repentance, seeking direction from God and learning to love one another. But, His message was not merely words, but one of demonstration, in that He demonstrated those things that He spoke of. He showed the ultimate power of God over sin and death. He ~~rose~~ died and rose from the dead. No prophet has ever done that. Only Jesus Christ.

Life or Liberty

Which is more important. Life or liberty. I would hate to choose. *Thank you, Jesus You have given both.* New life, new freedom. It's like a road we come across after wandering through the trees. It's not new, but new to us because we only just now found it. So, we merge with that road. It's one way. From behind to ahead. Eternity past to God only knows. But, we've merged. We weren't really on a marked trail. We had forged our own way through the bramble. We marched out from our place and then felt obligated to continue our way. Our own way. We just grabbed a machete and hacked away at anything stopping us. We had to get through. We had a goal, but it kept changing. New places seen over the next horizon. Yet, we never reached where we wanted to go. No, Thank you Jesus, we haven't. Those goals wouldn't have made us truly happy. He knows that the only true happiness is in life and freedom and His road is the only one that goes there.

Tornado Water

A sharp turn in the river causes an eddy. It is a place where the river flows and turns abruptly. Sometimes, in our lives, we turn quickly. We make sharp turns in the direction of God's will. He discloses a need and we respond. There are abrupt changes in our lives. Others see the eddy. The tornado of water, brought about by the turning of the life by the power of the Holy Spirit. And, believe me, they pause. For, everyone loves a water fall, a spin of whirling noisy water draws attention. An eddy flows around the rocks. For, the sand would quickly be eaten away. So, when we see someone who turns passionately toward God, notice, this is an eddy. A tornado caused by an abrupt change in the channel of his life. You can spot them. They are noisy.

Tornado Alley

A place where mighty circular wind touches down. Why do people live there? It's home. When the tornado comes, what needs to be rebuilt, is. We're the same. God's wind comes to us. His mighty voice touches down. What needs to be leveled, is. Then, we rebuild what should be in that place. By His grace. But, why do we live there? It's our home. It's us. Why wouldn't we leave? We are insured. His love, His provision. Eternal life with the Father, Son and the Holy Spirit. So, what's a few structures here on earth destroyed by wind?

It's like the three pigs. I guess they were not built strong enough to withstand the blowing.

Tornado of My Soul

Father, please stabilize my soul. I feel unbalanced, out of kilter, and undone. For, your Spirit has come through the center of a place I thought I had closed off. It was a place of very intimate pain. And I am not sure if I really Wanted you to go there. Now, that it is all in the open, I guess I will Ask for healing into that place of injury when I was a child, and my parents injured my soul, unwittingly, without intention.

Calypso

Upside down plan. I had a plan, but today, it went up side down. And, I know it was from God. He had led me. And I went. But, the response on the other side was not planned. He flipped the boat, capsized the plan, and over turned my dreams of the plans I had for his life. Calypso. It is a good thing Jesus specializes in turn overs because I need to turn this one over to Him. And, He needs to return to the situation and upright the progress of His plan. So, I will turn it over to Him. It's His anyway.

Some Men Cut on Me

Little by little, we who whittle, whittle. We slice away at the image of God that we hold within our capacity to reason. We cannot reason Him away completely, so we chip at Him. Just like a big block of ice, we take out our chisel and hammer of what we think He should look like. The problem with this is when the heat comes. Drought of our own lives. Then, this creation of ours melts. Just like an ice sculpture after the banquet. And, what is left inside continues to be there. The very image of God. No matter how small we have wished it to be, He lives on eternal. It was buried within all that ice. Good thing, for when the ice melts, we often need the only thread of hope that we held through that rough time.

Chiseled Image of God

Little by little, some whittle they cut God down. Make Him small, by making themselves big. They whittle away at His image until all they have is their own reasoning left. They attempt to reason Him completely out of their lives.

The Doubt Slide

God's answer is sandwiched somewhere between no, I think so, maybe, almost, sort of, perhaps, I hope so, and yes.

How did that happen? We once believed in the yes, then our faith slid. Like a cat standing on a newly waxed floor.

The feet gradually start to slide out from under him until he is unbalanced. The slide into doubt. There is no victory in doubt.

Doubt says, "I don't think so. Not much of a chance, the percentage of probability is extremely low for a positive outcome. It has never happened before. Who do you think you are? And, who is God to care about such things as these? You are inferior to Him, why would He care?"

See how the words of doubt slide?

Use the grace escape hatch and seek the truth about God and His Word. He does care. He does love. He has given over and over to make a way for us in the 'yes' modes. He is a 'yes' God. But, only through His power, and our faith to believe in His.

There is nothing to loose. But doubt.

God is a Recycler

He will not   waste any promise. When we make covenants of promise with Him, He remembers them and calls us to keep them time and time again. Maybe, we think our time is over, like an old Coke bottle drained of the beverage. But, God picks us up from the trash heap again and again. He makes new what we've disposed of. It's about covenants. Crushed glass often makes something beautiful. Old Coke bottles are often on display in a restaurant or, He could send us right back to where we left off. Refill us, and send us out again to be re-circulated. We just need a washing. Go to Him. Confess your sins. There's grace. Ask to be renewed in your covenants. He never threw you away, you laid down on that trash heap yourself.

Chancing Temptation

It is like we get too close to the edge of a place
we know we shouldn't be. The rim of the pit.

Judgment of Suicide

Devastation, destruction, and final judgment. One fell swoop has been declared by him. Devastation to the family who still questions reasons for his behavior and destruction of himself; the ending of his life. Stopping his own breath by his very hand. The gall of one who would do such a thing! Surely, there is judgment. And there is. For, he has merely sped up his own court date with his maker. Was he ready? Were his papers in order? Did he secure the lawyer? For, who will speak for him to God? And, what will he say to God? Imagine. How will he repent when he is already in heaven? How will he say he is sorry to those he, so miserably wounded, by taking his own life? There is no second chance for him. *God help him. For, we pray based on the timelessness of the eternal God, that he has been given predetermined grace to be ready for judgment. That he has claimed Jesus as his Savior, and as payment for his sins. So, that he may stand in the presence of God Almighty and not be found guilty for himself. Oh, that Jesus might stand for him as lawyer and the one who accepts his penalty. Oh, Dear Father, you knew his pain, like no one else. And, certainly, he cried out to you in agony in his final moments here on earth. Oh, Father may you grant his regrets. For, certainly, he prayed for me.*

Doubt

Threads of doubt weave the web where the spider lives. The black widow kills even her husband. There's no future in that relationship.
Doubt needs a way out of doubt.

Feeding on the Word

The cupboard is empty. All the food is gone. Empty abandoned and without. I can either stand there staring into the cupboard or go the table. For, when I sit at the table, food is delivered like a restaurant. That is the Kingdom of God. Our cupboards are empty. We don't have food. Jesus is our bread, our water, our wine, our meat. He is all we need. For, from Him come all the fruits of the Spirit. I don't like vegetables, anyway. But, when I sit at the table of His presence and ask, He brings all I need. His word comes to me on a silver platter with golden feet. Warmed and fresh his voice comes to meet my every need, above, and beyond. Forgiveness, reassurance of His love, healing, deliverance, and direction. Mercy brings us the platters of food over flowing with delicacies of His love. A feast for our souls.

Mocking Bird

Jesus paid the price to kill a mocking bird. For Satan mocks what is true. He has a whole line of counterfeits that mimic and mock the plan of God. He's a black bird that lacks creativity. For, when he departed from the plan God had for him, his wires that connected him to true creativity were snipped. Only God has the ability to make things new.

Prejudiced

The Dream:

My daughter's friends are weird. I don't understand them at first and I think they're rude. But, actually, it is me being prejudiced. We are freed when we dine together. That's when the wall comes down between us.

Interpretation:

My daughter represents the Church, the daughter of God reflected in many books of the Bible. The message of the dream is that sometimes we think that the daughters of our Father are weird.

We cannot associate with them because they are so different from us. God is saying to us that His friends are weird. But, so are we. When we both feed on the word of God and the presence of the Holy Spirit, the wall will come down that separates us. God will bring down the separation of the Churches when they feed on His presence. For, He is the peacemaker, the one who bridges the gaps between generations and nations. He is the one who brings us all together so that we will be able to worship as one body, the body of Christ. Because we all worship the same God, He is the one who will help us to understand each other. Just meet at the Cross. For, there we are all at the same level. Eye to eye, all at the feet of our Savior.

Trial and Err

It seems unfair that I should have a trial before I err. But, I do. I am found guilty of sin before I take my first breath. Then, I enter into sinfulness. My natural tendency is to err, go astray, veer off the right way. I am guilty either way. Lucky for me, there is a tireless arbitrator who speaks on my behalf; Who has access to the judge's chambers. Otherwise, I would be doing a lot of jail time.

Passive Thinking at the Core

The climax of the situation is a disagreement in thinking. Passive VS active. Fire either is, or isn't. Even a smolder is a fire that could flare up at any time. When we are passive, we by-pass the decision. When we by-pass the decision, we make no concise effort to decide the best option. We are like someone who defaults a race because we fail to run. We could have run, and we might have won the opponent. Satan has tricked us again, into believing we do not have an opponent. And, we thought we would win because the other team wouldn't show up. Every thought that opposes God's wisdom is alive and well. Like slime coming from a bad foundation, it oozes up from the ground we walk on. So, without even taking a stand to, or against, we will slip and slide and fall because our path has been coated with slime. Decisions that come from God's wisdom go to the bedrock of the foundation of the world, for He is the core of hole of creation. When we reach out to Him, and seek His leading in the decisions of our life, It's impossible for Satan to trip us up because nothing can come between this Father and His children. For The love of God is the core of the relationship. Values That stem from the core always prove true. For, true comes from Truth.

Switching Tracks

Why would you seek God with all your heart, soul, and strength? It's like throwing the brakes on a locomotive. The wheels lock up and the train screeches to a halt. When you seek God whole heartedly, all of the other things you have been doing screech to a halt. We stop doing the things we used to think were important. Something changes in our focus. We go from looking out the side window, to focusing forward down the track we are supposed to be on. And, when we do that we notice something on the tracks. At first, it's far off and we can't make it out. But, as it gets closer, and we come more near, we, suddenly, realize that there's a person tied to those tracks.

So, we throw on the brakes with everything we can. We stop our own training process. But, just like a locomotive, our life takes a while to be redirected. To stop what we were doing and start doing different stuff. That's a new track. We have to fully stop our old track before we can change to the other track.

We can see the change station ahead. It comes into view. All of the signs say change is coming. So, we go for it. We are not sure if we are going to change in enough time to avert the hazard, but we do. The master switcher has set the track for us ahead of time. And just in the nick of time, we get on the other track. We pass by the person tied to the rails only to see that she looks very much like ourselves, the hair is the same color. The skin tones are similar. She is wearing one of your outfits. They are clothes you recently gave away to the Salvation Army. In fact, she was you.

Eternal Wakefulness

It's late and I've been up for days. Awake to the impulses of the voice of the God who never sleeps. Oh, that we may get our flesh to sleep while our spirit stays awake eternally!

Reserve Grass at the Cross

Become empty, let go. Those things that you were hanging on to, need to be placed at the nail pierced feet of Jesus. When we refuse to bring Him our weights and sins, we are the ones who are the losers. It is like there is a field of grass at the foot of the cross where Jesus hangs. And, like a concert, God has a spot reserved for us in that grass. It's like a section where you would sit to watch a show. Only, it is at the foot of the cross. And, when Jesus calls us with reserve seats, we go to our spot. All front row tickets. We find our place there on the grass. It is there we face the cross, we face Him, drop our cares and pick up His. And, we have been given season tickets. These are ours for this season until He comes to take us home with Him.

Prayer Hike

It is our desire to go to the mountain of our God and meet Him in prayer. To climb the face of a mountain, we need rope and sturdy footholds. His position provides our footholds because when we are His Children, His position becomes ours by inheritance.

Jesus climbed the mountain first and left the pegs in the rock for us to use; to hold onto. The ropes are the Word to us today. Then there's grace if we slip, the safety rope. As we begin to climb the place of prayer that God has for us, we will begin to see His face as it truly is. We will come to know Him personally. We will come to know the rock, like a well traveled trail. The trail will open to us. It didn't move.

We just became familiar with it. It is as if the face of the mountain opens to us. The trail becomes our friend because we know it. As the face of the mountain opens to us, we realize that it is the face of God. It is His eyes that we begin to see things from. We start to develop His vision for others.

Keep Hiking

His attitudes, His love. He speaks to us, and we hear His voice because the trail is familiar to us. After we hike a trail for a while, we know where the blue birds live, We know where the deer drink, we know where the squirrels snuggle each other. We know, not only the way, but other things about it. We learn not only the ways of God, but other things about Him His face opens to us. His eyes open to us. His mouth opens to us. And, when His face opens to us, we find ourselves in the cleft, just as Moses was in the cleft. For, God opened His heart to Moses and Moses opened his heart to God. It was on the well traveled trail that they learned a new level of depth within their relationship. When we come to God through the blood of Jesus and to use the footholds He has provided, we can come up the face of God's mountain of prayer. It is a prayer hike.

Manifestation, Presence, and Life

Dream:

God showed me Father, Son, Holy Spirit. He gave me different manifestations of the Holy Spirit. I'm at work. Then, He will put all three back together in the future. Manifestation, Presence and life... are all the Holy Spirit

Interpretation:

The Holy Spirit comes to us. He manifests Himself in many forms; all the forms of God because He is God.

He Brings the Voice of God

His voice comes to our spirit in several ways. He may talk quietly, or loudly. Sometimes, even audibly. Then, there are times He shows us Himself. He gives us visions, dreams and physical manifestations.

He Brings the Presence of God

The Holy Spirit allows us to feel God; to know that He is here with us even though we cannot see Him. When the Holy Spirit brings the presence of God, once again He brings all the attributes of God to us. Often, we tremble, cry, and fall down when He shows up. He reveals God in the places where we need Him; to each of us individually.

He Brings Life

The Holy Spirit brings life. He is the breath. We can live, but without the Holy Spirit, we do not have life. It is the difference between standing and walking. We can stand when we accept Jesus as our Savior because He has become our brother. We stand with Him as we accept Him by faith. We have become acceptable to God through Jesus' blood for our sins. But, we can only walk by the grace of the Holy Spirit. The presence of the Holy Spirit gives life to our spirit breath, by breath. He is the breath that moves the body of God. He is the one that pumps the life into it by the power that He allows to flow. He shows us the heart of God and sustains that vision for us. He helps us to walk where we need to go.

A Vision

The picture He gave me is a large earthmover. Reverse Nuclear powered. Its power puts atoms together instead of apart. God is the driver, the power is the Holy Spirit and Jesus is the truck. It hauls all of the riches of God by the vehicle (Jesus). The cab is in the back. He is not in front of the riches, but behind them. It is large and powerful. The Spirit of Wisdom knows why the vehicle exists in its separate parts, unified. The Spirit of Understanding knows how it operates (physiology). The Spirit of Counsel reads the map to direct it. Power provides the Gas, the energy for the movement. The Spirit of Knowledge has the schemata of the truck (anatomy).

The Temptation of Jesus

The Kingdoms of Satan and God are shown in the temptation of Jesus in the desert. Jesus was taken to a place where there was no presence and voice of God. It was a dry place without water. There was no direction from God and no unity in power and presence.

In fasting, Jesus put aside His own flesh. He still had his will to contend with. Satan asked Jesus to make the stones into bread; To make bread on his own apart from the Father; to become his own presence and communion. Jesus refused to separate from the Father in the intended purpose to become a sacrifice for our sin. He was to become the bread, but at an ordained time. Jesus refused to create life. He had given up His dominion to the Father. He had separated from the Father. He refused to take back His role as Father.

The evil one challenged His sovereignty as God. He mocked the word of God against the power of God. The power evidenced by the rock and the word shown as a fragile Jesus who was hungry after 40 days of fasting. Then the Devil took Jesus to the highest point of the temple. The Devil could not go into the temple. He will be there at our highest point, ready to have us step out under our own strength to fall. He encouraged Jesus to use His own strength to keep from falling. Jesus refused to call on His own strength, but called on the grace of God in providing angels to keep Him from falling. Satan was mocking the dependence that Jesus had to exercise while on the earth. He had to become dependent on men, and on God, when, in fact He was God, himself.

Again, the Devil tempted Jesus. He took him to a high mountain. We go to mountains of prayer. We see the kingdoms that are unseen through the eyes of the spirit. We must look to the Holy Spirit to show us the unseen world. The Devil sees the unseen world, and he showed Jesus just how much of this world he has taken. I am sure it made Jesus sad to see how he had overrun the wills of men to hold them captive by his deception. He has his kingdoms set up everywhere.

He has infiltrated every aspect of our society here on earth. He wanted to make sure Jesus was aware of it. He was wondering if Jesus wanted to trade His hope of a future kingdom in for one now. He was trying to discourage Jesus from a future hope by showing Him how much power he has over men now. He claimed that he was willing to share this power with Jesus. He saw that Jesus had given up His power to become a man. Did He want some?

This was, no doubt, the first time Satan had seen God voluntarily lay down his power. God separated Himself to come to earth for us. He has brought us His Holy Spirit to give us His presence, His voice for direction, and life to the body. In the future we won't need these things because we will be with Him. He will scoop us up and take us with Him when He is joined all together again. What a glorious day that will be!

Isaiah 11, Matthew 4.

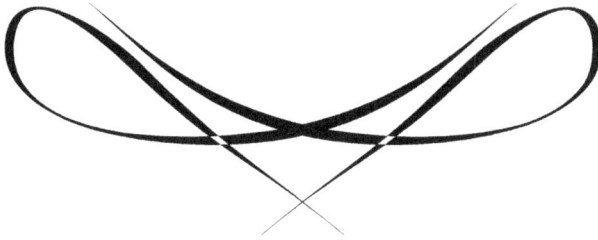

Prophecy Light

My light shines into their darkness to give understanding of what is ahead. Prophecy provides insight into the future. I long to give my people open eyes to see what is ahead. But, They Are Stubborn and insist on walking in the dark. Handcuffed.

Po Boy Righteousness

A poor boy doesn't ask for much because he doesn't know the options. Is God that way? Does He withhold blessings from us because we don't know to ask? How could He expect us to ask for things we have never heard of? If He says we don't have because we don't ask, then does He withhold? Is a father that way? Would He expect his son to know what to ask for? I don't think so. The compassion of God fills the gap between what we think we need and what we really need. We live within a covenant of compassion and grace. God is a loving Father who desires to give us blessing after blessing. He only asks us to be grateful, honor Him, and continue to have a personal relationship with Him. Easy. Just be a kid and let Him be the Father. Ask for your allowance.

Chapter II

His Kingdom Lives

The kingdom of God is built on a corporate love affair.

Sealed Operating Packages

Dream:

The Father wants to teach his son how stuff is sealed, so He seals some stuff up. It looks like sterile packages that are opened during surgery by the surgeon when he does surgery on someone. For operations.

When the Father brings them to the operating room, the operating room team gets mad because the packaging is not properly authorized. All supplies used in surgery need to be wrapped in sterile packaging after going through a long process of autoclaving. Then, when they are opened, the surgeon keeps all of the instruments sterile, so that the patient will not get infection during surgery.

The whole process has to be kept sterile. When the Father brings His packages, they question the sterility of the packaging, thinking that they are not properly wrapped by authorized persons trained in sterilizing of instruments, so they refuse them. They think that the packages are contaminated. So, they throw them on the floor of the operating room.

They don't understand the use of the packages. They think that they are for operating. Like the rest of the packages. But, they are not for operating, but for training the sons on how to operate. It is just for learning. The Father wants to teach his son about how things were sealed.

It's not about what he puts inside the sterile package, but the way the package is wrapped. It is like, when he gave those packages to his *son, He sealed a piece of himself in that package, so when they threw it on the floor, I was mortified.*

So, I get involved and they give me plans to sweep up. I tell the operating room staff that they don't understand and are not sensitive to the needs of the children to learn.

Interpretation:

The Father wants to give us training packages. They are like sterile packets of instruments used by a surgeon during surgery. He has provided a clean, sterile package with instruments tucked inside that can be used for operations. There are several different surgical packets available for whatever operation the surgeon needs to perform.

He can set bones, repair torn ligaments, remove cancer, or perform heart surgery. He can help deliver babies, stop internal bleeding, remove blood clots, and insert prosthesis where it is needed to allow the individual to walk.

When we think about the training that Our Father has for us, He does similar things in our life. He sets us upright, repairs torn places in our walk. He removes areas of bad growth, like a cancerous lesion, that form within us. He becomes a heart surgeon when He repairs our broken hearts and mends the areas of hurt. He is the one that delivers us from the enemy.

He also helps us to give birth to visions that He puts inside of us; in our womb. A vision is like a baby because it grows into maturity, then is born when it moves from being internalized to fulfilled. An artist has an idea, then, puts it on paper. The vision has been born. A song writer has a song, then, writes it. It has been born. A preacher has a message, then, writes it. The baby has been born. The baby matures, and grows. When the baby walks, that is when the preacher delivers the message to others. When the song writer sings the song, he walks into the vision allowing it to take feet to be carried to others. It has become a toddler.

We all have areas that need attention and repair. Our Father wants to be the surgeon to do the repair on our soul. When we join His team, it is like we are now in a HMO. It is a complete health maintenance organization. It is like He brings His team of experts that have complete knowledge about every area that needs help. He gives insight and healing where ever necessary. He will do the heart surgery, then, follow us through the rehabilitation program. He is the surgeon and the rehabilitation specialist. He becomes what ever we need because He already is whatever we need. He is just waiting for us to need Him in a certain way, so that when we do, He is already prepared to meet our needs.

The message of the dream is that our Father is moving outside of conventional methods of packaging to give us training. It is wrapped in sterile packages with a seal. The seal is the Holy Spirit. For, on Him God has set His seal of approval. It's like a seal of approval given to a package of goods sold in the grocery store. A company places their seal on a product indicating that they back this product behind their name. They approve of this product as if they had made it by their own hand. The Father has said this about Jesus. Then, Jesus said it about the Holy Spirit. After that, the Holy Spirit comes and seals us. The Father approves of Jesus as if He were Himself. He backs Jesus with His name, the name of God Almighty.

The Holy Spirit is given by Jesus to us as His seal of approval on us. It is like a stay fresh seal on the Tupperware to keep us fresh until the day that we will be made complete in His presence in heaven. It is like a lid over our heart. It locks in the freshness of God's word for today.

Jesus gave us the Holy Spirit to be our companion until we are carried to heaven. He is given to us as a guarantee of the real thing. He is like the pink slip on a car that might be given to the new owner before the car is delivered. We hold the pink slip.

The difference between the pink slip of a car and the Holy Spirit, is that He is God. He is every aspect of God combined in a package that is made to live within us while we are here on earth. Just like the Ark of the Covenant in the Old Testament, He is the lid of the package. He brings His presence with mercy.

The Ark of the Covenant was a box that Moses was instructed to build so that the new country of Israel could worship God. It was a portable church, so the box was carried from place to place as they traveled around claiming the new territory that they were given. The lid of the box was called the mercy Seat. It was what sealed the box, closed the lid, enabling the covenant to be closed.

The Holy Spirit is given to us by God's mercy, to seal the deal between Him and us. The giving of the Holy Spirit is the final act of God's mercy to His children.

When we invite the Holy Spirit to help us, we open the seal of His mercy covenant with us. Our Father comes flying in on the wings of the dove and acts within our situation with mercy to cap His promises. He brings the provision to the promises.

Remember the dream? The tools for surgery are tucked within the surgery packet, sealed tight with a sterile seal. Sometimes, we don't recognize the package that the Father gives us. In the dream, the operating team throws it on the floor, trampling it under their feet in disrespect.

There is confusion as to the purpose of the packages. The operating team thinks the packages are used for surgery. They are not to be used for surgery. God has not given us instruments to perform surgery on each other. I do not have the instruments to evaluate your sickness and heal you. I do not have the instruments to mend your broken heart or remove the cancer from your life. We do not have this power. God has not given us this kind of package.

We are only to break the seal, then, He will come to perform the surgery Himself. When we invite the Holy Spirit into our lives, He will bring healing, deliverance, and salvation. We do not need to try to bring healing into others' lives. We are to urge them to break the seal, themselves and ask God.

The tools within the packages that God provides are the gifts of the Holy Spirit. He provides whatever we need for that time, that surgery, that incident. If someone needs healing, when we pray, the gift of healing is within the packet. We simply break the seal on the OR package and let Him work. We bring out the gift of healing and pray it in. He does the work. It is His Spirit working into their lives.

The Father wants to teach His children how to rely upon the Holy Spirit to be their teacher. That is what the OR packages are for. Everything God is; is within those packages because He paid the delivery charge by sending Jesus, His Son to die for us.

John 3.33, 6.27, 16, II Corinthians 1.21-22, Ephesians 1.13-14, Revelation 5.9.

Fling Seed

Make the prayer bigger. Prayer is like seed.
Pretend you are the one spreading grass seed.
Would you put it in a little pile close to you?
Would you use a mechanical spreader?
Would you use a tractor?
No, for you spread
grass seed by hand.
You spread it, then go back
over the areas to make sure you didn't
miss any. A mechanical process will not work.
God wants to move His voice through our hand.
The tractor will leave ruts and tracks that no seed
can be planted in. It will ruin the whole process.
No, you stand in one spot and fling the seed.
Pray and twirl.
Spin around and around with as much
seed as you can carry to pray for as
many as possible. Pray the Word
of God. If we pray for one
person, why not include
his wife. And, if his
wife, why not the
kids. And their
kids. You see,
fling   the
seed.

Twirl.

Mercy Prompts Miracles

Tenderness abounds where mercy resounds echoing in our time of need. O precious gift from God given by the Holy Spirit to show His love to His children lined with faith, tender mercy prompts miracles. Because the faith opens the door in a place that used to be not there. It was a wall, a stone fence, a hole, a web. Until His provision came bursting through and shed light on the dark situation. The vision to a miracle looks to the light even though it might not be turned on yet. Maybe, we haven't even found the light switch.

But, still, we know that He wouldn't build a house and not put light fixtures in it. So, we go into that room. We have to feel for the light switch. The feeling is done with our heart to His.

Power and Might

What is the difference between power and might? Power is the flow of the Holy Spirit. God does not give his Spirit by measure. If we have the Holy Spirit, we have all of Him. Might is the force. The press. The degree of pressure as from a valve. It is like a valve that releases the gas into the engine to make more power. The potential for the release was always there, but the valve needed to be opened to release it. How do we get it? The valve needs to be turned sideways to open up for the might to be released. We need to lay down. Turn our heart toward Him. Open up. It is like when the wing is pulled in toward the F14, it decreases the drag and the jet flies faster. The power was always there, But had not been released Because the flaps were in the way. We must become flat before God. Flatten ourselves. We are in the way of the release of the power; Might. Our valves are stuck. They are junked over with our own grime. We need to use soap and a brush. Scrub.

Eternal Spa

Where are you, Girl? The spa, the mall, the party? Why? A massage, new stuff, happy feelings? Let Me know when you burn out, for I will provide eternal beauty, a royal house ever more, and joy enduring. My heavenly spa, My bottomless blessings, and My glorious inheritance of eternal happiness in the presence of God. Just let Me know.

Singing Echo

One sung heart, sung to another tunes of affection,
love eternal. Now two hearts sing because one heart sung
and the other did the echo.

Advancement of the Kingdom of God

Ministry is the display of God's heart to others. When His heart is shown to us, moves through us and flows to them, we have moved into ministry. He is the one who trains us because only, He knows, what is on His heart. Training is not done by us or by the Church.

What is the role of the church, then, Lord?

To convert.

But, I thought it was to advance the Kingdom of God.

Wrong. You do not advance My Kingdom, I do. For you cannot make the clock move forward. It is like moving the sea shore. You cannot make it move. It moves by the seasons. The times. And I dictate the times and the seasons. Your job is to do what I tell you. When you do your job, there is an advancement of My purposes and presence in the lives of others. Advancement of My Kingdom is done through worship. You become a symbol of worship when you Worship Me in front of others. They see it and magnify Me. My Kingdom is advanced. You are My hands, but not My voice. You are to listen to My voice, echo and obey.

Freedom Demonstration

The Dream:

I am driving my car around a block. It turns out to be further than I suspected. I end up in the middle of a freedom fight. It is a demonstration and they are all walking my way. I attempt to turn around and am unable because there is a median. There is no off ramp. It is a one way road. It looks like nearly everyone else is going the other direction.

The scene backs up and I see myself in the car. My car, along with some other cars, and a bus are 'buckled in' on the freeway with a large belt. There are earthquakes and bombs going off all around, but in the midst there are some of us who are secure as we stay on the way, going the direction that we are supposed to be going, even though it is contrary to the others. We are bound by a large tie, like a belt. Even though I am in the midst of a freedom fight, a large demonstration, I don't get hurt. There are people, casualties all around. Blood splatters my windshield. I don't get harmed by the demonstration.

Then, God said, "You and I are joined together in the midst of a huge demonstration."

Interpretation:

God has given me insight to drive the vehicle that He has given me around a block in my life. As I get into the vehicle, the gift, that He has provided, He will give me insight to see over the blocks of the enemy. There is a big demonstration of His power when we do things using the gifts He has given, calling upon the power He provides.

Some times I may feel like I am in the middle of a big war; a freedom fight, but I can't back down. I have come too far to turn back now.

He has buckled me inside of my car on His free way. He is the way, the truth and the life. His way is the only way to get freedom. He provides the buckle that holds the whole program in.

There is a huge fight between the powers of God and the powers of Satan, but God has promised to protect me in the midst of it. It is like being in the middle of a war, or a demonstration, full of violence.

When I go His way, it will seem like I am going the wrong way on the freeway. Some will think I am drunk, perhaps. I guess, I am. Drunk in the Holy Spirit. And, He promises to provide everything I need to go against the system that the world has provided to make it seem like people are being sent on the free way. But, God will show them, through these writings, that He has provided another freeway, the way of hearing His voice above the din of the other things in their lives. He has made a way for a joining of our heart to His amidst the anarchy of the freedom battle. *Malachi 3.1, John 14.6, Hebrews 10.20*

First and Last

How can God be the first and the last, yet there are those who don't seem to notice? They live their lives as if they are in charge. As if they have the first and the last say of life.

Contemplation Revolution

Contemplation, revelation, resolution, revolution. For, when we contemplate the truth, He will reveal Himself. When we resolve to follow that truth, there will be a revolution. Be resolute, be firm, be sure. Stand on the rock. When we stand on that rock, Jesus, our clay feet become as brass. Wave a banner, fly a flag. Be a drape to be pulled back from the windows that allow the light from heaven to shine in. We are a banner raised to be unfurled against the bow. Hold God to His promises and He will.

Revival and Revolution

What difference is there between light and life? Debt and death? Understanding and intuition? Revival and revolution? With light we can see where we are going. With the life we can get there. Debt is what is due to God from us because of our position. Our final payment is death. Death to the dream, death to our ideas, death to us. Through the Holy Spirit we have not merely intuition, but understanding of God's Word, will and ways. Of how Jesus is the light came to pay our debt, give us life in exchange for death and insure understanding of the Kingdom of God. As we move from the feeling of intuition into assurance, then we step from 'I think so' into faith. Our 'maybe' becomes our 'yes' through Him. He will sustain His 'yes'. That's when we will find ourselves amidst a revolution.

Hope Whispers Your Name

Whispering hope calls your name.
Wait till the morning is over, after the morning is lost.
Oh, how close My Hope calls your name.
Justice to over come and plan of evil doth swindle.
Whispering hope.
Oh, how close My Hope calls to you, my love.
Brightness presses in where the night has ebbed in.
My sun streams through the window into the table setting
of My presence.
A presence of love and mercy
for those I have called out by My name.

Whisper of Hope

Soft as a voice of an angel,
Gently He calls to my name.
Sweet is the voice of my Savior.
Drawing Me to His proclaim.

Wait till the night time is over,
Wait till the morning is passed.
Once in the dawning discover
Hope, blessed Hope, that will last.

Whispering Hope, oh how wonderful, wonder to me.
Calling my name, not the same,
May I pause, just because
His sweet love, Eternal Dove, draws me nigh unto Thee.

Hope for the brightness tomorrow,
Once this dank day is done.
Sweet, tender mercy, no sorrow,
Love kisses sweet, to dear one.

Whispering Hope, oh how wonderful, wonder to me.
Calling my name, not the same,
May I pause, just because
His sweet love, Eternal Dove, draws me nigh unto Thee.

(This was given to me as a song in the night to the tune of an old
hymn called *Whispering Hope*.)

Kingdom of Love

Wisdom, honor, power and might flow from the one and only God who was and is and is to come. Lord of all. Wisdom to know what is absolute. The honor of Being the absolute ruler of the universe. Power unsurpassed. And might that flows from His heart unleashed freely to all who believe. He rules with love. We have never seen a kingdom on earth ruled with love. All have Other motivations. That is why we have such a hard time understanding it.

Eternal Kingdom

When did we think forever was only a little while? When we stopped looking with our spiritual eyes and started seeing everything as temporal. It is only the world that passes away. We pass on. On, through, to. On to Jesus, through His blood, to the new Kingdom. I believe it will be heaven on earth.

Never Ending Recess

I hereby release My people to have unbridled joy. Parameters substantiate the distance between two points. Here and there. When we allow God to set the grid lines, then we can have all the fun we want. There is safety within His playing field. He is the yard guard, the security, the principle and the teacher. The bell does not ring before we are ready to go in, When the kids decide how long recess takes. Join in with Him In the never ending recess. Find the rest for our soul. Let Him set The parameters.

Appropriations Committee

The appropriations committee has met before the start of time and set aside everything we need for our stay on earth. When we learn how to live within the boundaries He has set, there will always be provision.

Army of One

The throat of the enemy is reality. My Word cuts the throat of the enemy. Welcome to war. Over, above around and through I will be victorious with you. Put your hand in Mine. For together we form the army of One. My vision, with your eyes. My direction, with your feet. My power, with your frailty. My show of love, your show of obedience. The enemy has no weapon formed to come against My love. He is way out numbered, out powered, out witted. Three to One.

A Damned Piece of Clay

Satan is spirit. He is not flesh. He is an angel. He is eternal because that is the track I set him on. He has no intention for himself. He is at the mercy of the potter, for he is a formed vessel, a damned piece of clay.

Pitter Patter, Heart Claim

Pitter, patter. My heart beats for You alone. I can feel it racing into yours. Tremble, melt, become like water. The coo of His voice causes my heart to come alive. Shake, quake, melt, become molded like water flowing over the top. What joy, overwhelming joy to be in love with my Savior Divine. When He comes, He doesn't waste any letters. *I proclaim. I stake my claim Before I claim. It was before I said, as I said, it will become.*

Rocks in the River

We think the rocks in the river are to dam, to hold us back. We see bad experiences as stumbling stones. But they are really a place for water to pool up and overflow. The water is the Holy Spirit. Where we are the weakest, He fills the most.

Where we need Him, He meets us at that point of need. So, where there are rocks, the water backs up to overflowing causing a waterfall. There is a mighty crash of water as it rushes swiftly down the ravine to its destination, the sea. There will be a back up of water for a while. Sometimes we worry, because we feel like we are backed up against a wall with no way out. We are afraid that the problem has won the victory over our lives. But, God wants to work His greatest show of power through our greatest needs.

The bigger the need, the bigger the meeting will be. It will result in a larger show of His power and greatness. It is like a magnificent water fall. The testimony will continue to flow and all will see and hear it, just like crashing water.

The things that we 'dam', God wants to use to overflow Himself. To get to that place of victory, however, we need to face the things that we have damned in our lives. We need to return to those areas of hurt, and allow His grace to come with healing. He is cool water, like an ice pack on a fractured bone, and He will cleanse and refresh in ways that are beyond our imagination. For, God alone brings absolute victory.

His definition of victory is when we are not afraid to return to any place along the trail of our lives because we have been there before. God has walked inside our hearts to take us there before now.

You, see, He goes in front of us preparing the way. He is the cook in the kitchen who prepares the turkey for Thanksgiving dinner. We just come along and put it into the oven. He has already been up for hours preparing the stuffing and basting.

Back Track

Back track needs to be the track behind you. Let it go.
It was your rail before, but not today.

Pruning Season

The more we let Him prune us, the more flowers we will have.
Sometimes we get pruning season mixed up with the blooming.
Sometimes there's both. O Rose of Sharon.

Showing our Bloomers

For your bloomers to show, you have to take off your skirt.
It's OK. Go to the dressing room. There's one waiting for you.
It's left by the Lamb.

Be Healed

Be healed O sweet Children.
Your pain has more than crossed my mind.
Believe me. I know, and I am known by my Father.
Ask Him.

A Bad Tour Guide

At the entrance to the kingdom there is a woman who makes
money. She is a fake. She scams and undercuts the tours.
She sleeps in a place of her own opulence, but in the
morning, she comes to meet those in need as they
attempt to enter the place of fun with God. She gives
them a ride, telling them not to walk the way God
wants them to go. She becomes their driver. She
drives with their need to find a fun filled place.
They have come to find God in a fun way,
And she   diverts their attention. They
forget why they are there, and get
sidetracked with the fun   instead
of seeking God. She drives them through the park
without stopping and keeps the profits. She steals
God's glory for herself. For the passengers
are marveled at her ability to lead
them into the fun place. But,
they never get out
of the car. She
never lets
any of
their
feet
touch the
ground of the place
they originally intended to see;
the Kingdom of God.
She is not
supported
by the management,
for she gives her own tours.
She feeds off those who want to
find 'fun' in the Kingdom of God.
She is a party spirit, just passing through
for a good time. These have gotten sidetracked
with her and never step one foot inside the Kingdom.

Low Walls, made High by Us

Walls are, really, many times a matter of perspective. For,
if your are standing at the bottom of a hill, and look up
at a wall, it looks big. But, as you walk up the hill
Towards the wall, it becomes smaller. A wall that
is only a few feet tall can look towering from an
angle below. I had that happen yesterday. For,
when I spun around, I saw a huge towering
wall standing between the plans I had been
given By God and the fulfillment of them.
And, for a time, the wall was tall. For, I
had placed it on a mountain of thinking
within my own strength. I approached it
from a certain direction. Like attempting to climb a
hill by going up the face. Even though the hill may
be a low elevation, if I attempt to get to the top by
going straight up the cliff, I won't be able to.
What we do, often, is go home and dig our
ropes out of the closet and
come back
to the
face
of the
rock
and climb
it our own way.
We forget that the hill has
more than one side to it. We need to stop
and ask God for His perspective. For, He promises
to meet His plans with His provision. Not ours. That
same hill can easily be approached from the back side.
And, He will show the way. It is easy going His way.

Lemon Delight

The plans of God have seeds in them that build other things.
They are like the miracle of the feeding of the five
thousand. The bread keeps multiplying as long as
they continued to break it. When He provides
a vision, and we keep coming back to
Him to develop it, He will multiply it
much larger than we had ever dreamed of.
It is like He gives a pie to us. It can be sliced
into unlimited pieces because each piece has seeds
that would grow another one. The seeds for ministry
are for us as well. When we step into what He wants,
we will be the one who is the most ministered to. We
will be blessed as He leads us through areas of our lives
that we have been broken and defeated in the past to
overcome; be victorious living within His grace.
His grace will be on display within the ministry.
He will show His love to us. The very things
that have brought the deepest hurts
are the areas that He will bring
the most healing. It will
fill up and overflow to
others within the
boundaries
of His
plan
for
healing in their lives.
Mincemeat pie
Will be
turned
into
lemon delight. When we have
become healed and made victorious, then we
will be ready to serve others. We envision victory,
then live it, to be convincing to others that it is for them.

A Great Victory

Amazing love that causes us to be intertwined with so great a victory. The defeat of all of the enemies of God, Almighty! The enemy has no weapon formed to come against My love. He is way out numbered, out powered, out witted. Three to One.

Peace Floods

Distress and agitation bow when peace shows up because peace comes in like water flooding from the place that has over flowed up from the basement level.

We Do, by Done

Because I said, "I do."
There is a marriage of ideas.
We join hands and walk down to the altar.
Because, before you were, We said.
Your did, is done.
It's ours. Done, finished.
Our plan, our power, your prayer, your obedience, our walk.
Jesus, The first word, the last word.
Alpha and Omega.
Beginning and end.
The plan, the provision, the proof.

What if Jesus Whispers

What if Jesus comes back and He doesn't make a big show of
it? What will happen then? Suppose He doesn't come in the
clouds with grand splendor, so as to drown out the noise of
other things we have going? Suppose He just comes back
to call us to Himself with a quiet voice. Suppose He
whispers His song of hope into our ear, like a tune
gently hummed to a baby. Then, He only takes
to heaven those who hear Him. He leaves the
rest behind. Would we hear Him? Is our ear
tuned to hear His humming? What are we listening to?
For, certainly there is nonstop noise within our world.
Even when we decide to get away, turn the television off,
and hide from our job, still, do our own thoughts make
so much noise, we do not allow our Lord a word in?
But, what if He drops down from heaven one day,
and stands in the middle of our city, and
declares that all who hear His voice
can go home with Him; All who
did not, are left behind. Oh,
we know that, surely,
the voice of the
Savior
would cut through to the heart.
It would
be like a
special song
that causes our spirit to be moved.
Certainly, our spirit would notice He was near.
But, is our ear attentive to His voice? I'm not sure.

Sharing Hope

I shared my Jesus today. They were hurting. They had
been told that she would die. I told them they were
wrong. Oh, it took all day. But, as I demonstrated
the true love of God and permitted Him to touch
my heart along with theirs, they came to trust me.
When they trusted me, then they trusted my words.
And, it was then, that I spoke what God had put on
my heart. I gave them hope. For, the doctors had told
them she would die. So, they were without hope and in
despair. But, it knew she was a Christian. And, a Christian
is never without hope. The Second verse came to me. God said
that with wings of eagles she would mount up, if she waited
on His timing for healing. The healing timing was not
dependent on anyone else, but God. And, she is
not terminal. She has had long illness.
But,
why would
we give up hope?
It is wrong to give up hope
when there is hope in God.
Our hope is not in men.
If our hope is
in them,
we are
the
most
to be pitied.
But, we don't
trust in doctors or
nurses or our own grit.
Our hope is in Jesus
Christ.
He is our only hope.
Her healing will come because she
has faith in Jesus. So, even if she is taken
from this world, she has the ultimate Hope.

Ultimate Hope

For, then she is in His very presence. So, once again I learned an important lesson: Don't let anyone take your hope. It is not theirs to take. Hope belongs to God. It's His, not ours. For, in Him alone is all hope, and there is none apart from His. So, I shared My Jesus, the hope giver, with the despaired family. And they, once again, saw that He is. She was not healed today, but she will be. Because He said so. If we are not totally healed, He is not done yet. For, we will all be perfect one day. That is our absolute hope, only found in the one true God, our Father in Heaven, the Lord Jesus Christ, the Hope of Glory, Eternal and Immortal. It's nice that He happens to, also, be my Father.

Hope Vendor

Father, I want to be a hope vendor. Someone who stands on the street corner passing out hope to anyone who will accept it. Like a street vendor who passes out fliers, I will yell of Your goodness And scream of Your mercy. Until all of my fliers are gone for the day. Until there isn't any more. And, I know that is impossible, though, because, You are the one who gives the hope. Just like the distributor of the newspapers, the delivery of your hope and mercy will continue. So, Father, I pray for endurance to do the job that You have assigned me to. To man the corner of my block and pass out hope day after day to any hands that reach out and accept it. Because, without Your hope, then we are hopeless. There is none to deliver, none to save, none to help us in our misery. Take pity on your people, dear Lord, and give us Hope. Amen

Ring Around the Rosary

I was there when she gave her heart to Jesus With a rosary,
she committed herself to Him. I simply held her hand. And,
as we gathered around that rosary in the presence of the Holy
Spirit, His power flooded the hospital room. Her lung cancer
shrunk in her mind when she relinquished her rights. And, she
used her final breaths for three prayers. They joined hands like
children who play ring around the rosary. We held hands. Her
with me, me with Him, Him with her. With three Catholic
prayers, sent to her by the Holy Spirit, her mouth moved
on it's own. For, she was not Catholic. She had never
learned those prayers. As I lent her my rosary bracelet,
and joined hands, the Holy Spirit moved on her
and out of her mouth came her heart's desire.
Miracle
I didn't understand the magnitude of
then, but I felt the power of God
released. He showed up because our
hearts reached out to him with honesty.
But, the most amazing thing was that He used
her lips to say prayers she had never learned. For,
as I spoke in tongues, she became the interpreter. Amazing.
She is Episcopalian.
Our Father, Hail Mary and Contrition.
What was I to say now that she said all
the important ones?
My tears pooled
at the place
on my
neck,
where
my own gold cross hung.
For, they were spilling over my mascara,
across my cheeks and joined hands under my chin.
Like a small creek, they ran and ran. For, I felt her
agony. Her kiss of death met with the kiss of compassion
that only comes through the cross of Jesus on that rosary.

53

More Rosary Prayer

That is why He is still on it. Because, He continues to
Minister to us from that place. What was left for me
to say? The blessing. So, I used the only breath I had
left, to call upon His grace given to us by His rosary
and our rosary. And, I saw her spirit join with Him,
for she gave it away. And, they scurried around her,
thinking she would die any moment. They saw the
peace on her face and recognized it as infatuation
with the one who brings us into His presence
in Heaven. And, it was true. But, she is still
here. And, in fact, she's better. Because
God granted her a window of healing.
He gave her unity and grace, peace
and deliverance from her pain.
And, her husband, now
in his eighties, took
his wheel chair and went to church this
morning. It was the first time in ten years he
had been to church. And, nobody can shut her
daughter up, for she is telling everybody
about the miracle of healing that has
come to her mother through
the power of the
resurrection
that is
represented
on   the   rosary.
So, I sang to her today, and
she grew more in love with that rosary
for what it represented. Unity with Christ,
encircling love, and   prayers properly aligned
the glory of God met with contrition and overwhelmed
with His grace again and again. A circle of His love.

54

Garden of His Expectation

He has a garden. We are grown in it. Grown in the garden of His expectation. For, He has dreams, too. Like us, and He longs to see us become successful. He wants to see us become the plan.

Mounds of Joy

Mounds of joy like mounds of snow for children to play in float to earth. One by one and meet in the park piled by the wind. Our heavenly Father provided the snow flake by flake high in the heavens above our head, then sent it for the children to play in. He knows they need some depth, so He puffs His cheeks a bit and gathers it in a place where they meet. The God I know plans such events. For, He made the earth and all that is within it for our delight. So, He knew when He formed those snow flakes, exactly where they would fall. Then, He knew exactly how hard to blow the wind to pile it up for them. Because He plans ahead to provide us with experiences that bring us delight and joy. *Father, thank you for providing us with delight in nature. I'm sorry I have been so slow to say thank you. But, here I am. And I say thanks.*

Power Transfer

There's been a transfer of power. The body is sandwiched between Trusting in Jesus and knowing when to come to a different channel. Whose not healed? Gather them up and help them trust God for a miracle. Do you want a piece of the pie? Let's share it with the kids.

Midnight Lover

Midnight lover awake because I can't sleep. My soul dances as my spirit plays music to the tune of the one I love. Ballet with Jesus. Twirl, leap, pirouette, dive, dip, laugh, and raise your glass to toast. To Us. The happy couple. Congratulations. It's a holiday, a Happy occasion. A reunion. A High School Reunion. School of the Most High God. He's given the letters and passed out awards. We've walked the halls, now He waits for us to walk the isle. To put on our gown. I have yet to graduate. It will come in His time. The tassels of Hope hang where we can see them. There's fresh plans for the future, but I'm afraid that I've been sent to graduate school. Guess I'll get a new computer.

Corianta' Apple Pie

My soul sings for the one I love. There is a combination that brings us to a place where God is able to drop us into His situations, knowing we have everything we need to respond, enabled by His grace, to bring Him praise. What is the Corianta' combination, Lord?

You are cored out, like an apple. Let Me explain: You come To Me, ask Me to be your Savior, and dedicate your life to serving Me. Then, I grow you, like an apple tree. I feed and weed. Put you into the soil, the nurturing of My hands, to make you sturdy in your walk. I point out things that are crowding Me out.

Weeds like ministry, family, church activities. These things crowd My personal time with you. I show you when you are crowding your space with Me by other things in your life. As you begin to lift Me up, elevate My name, I begin to lift you up. Seasons pass and your roots deepen in My love. For, I have a tree of love that grows nearby. I curiously watch as you begin to bud, then blossom, the fruit from the places where you extend your self using the gifts I have provided.

The tree of love provides the cross Pollination for your tree which permits it to produce succulent apples to make apple pies, caramel apples, and cobbler to be served to My children. As your fruit matures, and you start to show love, joy, peace patience, kindness, mercy, and gentleness. The apples cannot be put into the pie whole.

They need further preparation. I give gifts of the Holy Spirit that flows up through the sap Of the tree. It is contained in the vital fluids. Then, you must stand still and let Me pick from all that fruit. It's like being at a train station. Let Me pick the train. For, if you pick the train, then the destination will be 100 miles from where you are supposed to be. There is a time of specialized training for the ministry, I have intended for you to have. That is the Season of ripening. The apples picked too soon, will give children a stomach ache. So, train and wait. Wait on My timing.

Train with Me. Learn to Listen for when your train comes to your station. We all have specific stations in life. I train you for them. But, still, you are not arrived at the destination of your Corianta'. The apple must be cored. What you have centered your existence on, needs to be taken out. All of your ideas of what you want to do, where you want to go, and how to get there, need to be left in my kitchen, cored out by mother Wisdom. And it's not a trade. For, an apple is merely on it's way to becoming it's intended purpose when it is cored. More waiting. But, now we wait on mother Wisdom to prepare us with Her own hand. For, we are in the kitchen of the master, the gardener, the life that feeds the tree.

And, she pares us. She pairs us with the Holy Spirit in a matrimony, union, a merge with a knife, that cuts to our soul. Eternal indentions with no intent to wound, but, rather to change the form of the fruit so that is dessert for the family of God. The most important ingredient added at this time is sugar. Sweetness. Stirred in sweetness by the Holy Spirit as He stirs our heart in the table of His presence. Now, you are ready to sing. For, Corianta' is your core removed and, My song implanted within that place.

Remember, sour apples are not ready to serve. Sour faced individuals; they have jumped off the tree, gotten on the wrong train too early. It's a sign of impatience. It's up to us to show them the opposite. Not patience, but temperance. Apple pie can Be served any where anytime heated, cooled, with ice cream, with whip cream, to those cutting teeth, and to those whose teeth don't fit.

God can use our gift anytime He wants. You have become His sweet surprise, His hidden delicacy. A taste temptation that is always ready to serve. God likes apple pie warmed and served with love at His table.

Fudge Cake

The Dream:

The sweetness of the Holy Spirit is like a triple layer fudge cake.

Interpretation:

What God has for us is above anything we can think or even dream. He will be nothing but sweetness to our soul. Our soul will come to Him just like a humming bird if we allow it to seek Him. We can eat and eat and eat off of the sweetness that He offers to us. He is triple layer. Father, Son and Holy Spirit all in one cake. He has layers; three parts, but all baked into one desert. His presence to us is not merely bread, water, milk, and wine, but He will provide the desert for us if we stay. He wants us never to leave. He wants us to be fat. It is the fatness that breaks the yoke. The yoke of the enemy on his children. As we stay in His presence and get fat, then we will pick up what He has for us to do and He will make us into yoke breakers.

I guess, to make a cake, a lot of yokes need to be broken. The cake in my dream was very rich. Full of chocolate, oil, and eggs. Seeds of the Kingdom and the word of God, oil of the Holy Spirit and evidence of broken yokes. Hooray!

Sweet Miracles

If we do nothing else, call on Him to work miracles in our lives because of His love. The wrappers are His love cushions. For, it is the love is what keeps The sweetness in its place within the gifting of the Holy Spirit. *How I love you, my dear children. I wish For your sweetness. For in the sweetness I can share.*

The Boat

That which floats us to the place we are meant to be is like a boat. The boat is praying into the love of God with faith in the gifts of God believing Him For Who He says He is.

Galleon Flag Ship

A menu for my date. Lunch on the veranda. Son shine under the umbrella. Watch the flowers climb on the trellis. Chose a table next to the sea shore. Hear the sea. Look to the horizon A ship is coming over the horizon. A galleon ship. The aye, aye captain. The one who always says yes when we come to him. It's a ship with five sails.

It must be driven by grace. Mercy; She's the woman on the bow. She parts the water. The wind will drive that ship into our harbor. My The harbor and anchor it in the safe harbor. You could get on the ship by the dock, but it does not come into shallow water. It needs to stay in the deep places. I have to take a smaller boat to get out to it.

Cups

The dream:

There was a granite wall like one on a government building. The words were carved into the side of the wall. I saw the words, then, read them. The Words, "Clear the way for the people: Take the cups out of the way."

Interpretation:

There is a government that has buildings just like our government, only it is in a spiritual Kingdom. The structures there are just as real as the ones that we find downtown at the courthouse.

God is the inscriber of the messages written on the buildings in this Kingdom. He has a building dedicated to clearing the way for us. What does it hold?

We have in our hand everything that we have worked for. We have education, up bringing, religion, family pride, standing in the community and position in our jobs. We have many things that we hold dear to our hearts. We hold our families, our friends and our Church close to our hearts. We have dreams and goals for what we want to accomplish and what we want our children to accomplish. We have desires for what we would like our ministry to become. There are numbers and agenda within those numbers that we would like to achieve within specific time periods.

We are goal oriented. School is held within certain months and when we have gone 12 years, we are expected to graduate. Then, we are expected to be finished with college within an assigned date. If we fall short of these goals, then those around us start to ask questions of why we did not finish within that time.

What are we holding in our hands? Really. Do we have control over our own lives? Can we actually fulfill our own goals, or are they merely dreams that will never come true?

We need to separate what is in God's hands from what is in our hands. God has the ability to control the future.

He has all power and might. So, what do we have? We have the ability to let go. Often, we are wresting God for plans for our lives. We want to make our ideas succeed. We don't go to him in the planning stages, but wine to him when they don't work out. The dream calls us to clear the cups. To give up what we are holding onto. We need to give him our aspirations, our goals and our lives. When the table is cleared, then he can set before us what we are intended to have. He created us for a specific purpose and only He knows what that is.

Perhaps, we have been drinking from a soup bowl when he wants to provide a tea cup. Our hand may be better fitted to a tea cup. Maybe, we should have a mug instead of a pitcher. When we let go of what we hold onto, then our hands will be free to do what he has intended them to do.

Four years ago, I devised a wonderful plan to develop a 'free medical clinic'. I did all of the planning, was given an office space and instructed to work out a budget. I had physicians who were willing to donate their time all lined up. I did this plan, then, gave it to God. I remember looking at that packet as it sat under the pastor's chair and committing all of it to God. I let go of it.

I have never talked about it to Him since. I have never opened that packet. God used my willingness to develop that plan, to give me discipline to turn me into a writer. If I had pushed through the plan of becoming a director of a medical clinic, then I would not have become what God had intended for me to be. I let go of the cup. I cleared it out of the way and made a way for the plan that He intended for me. I try to give away everything I hold in my hand to God about twice a week. That way He can give bigger stuff.

Often times we are content with a plastic table cloth and plastic silverware when God has a storehouse of china and linen waiting for us. We must let go of the plastic and tin so there is room on the table for what He has for us.

Savior Complete

Everlasting faithfulness is mine through the provision of the Divine Savior. He is, and was, and is to come. Faithful, and true, Savior complete

Christmas Bulbs

Tulips Grow virtually every color of My Rainbow from bulbs planted in the spring in fertile soil. Bloom for Me. Be My fragrance. Display My true colors. My Christmas lights for the Nations Bulbs of many colors A holy nation. My People adorned with the light of the knowledge of who I Am. Eternal God, everlasting Savior, King Of Kings, Lover of your Soul God lives To exalt His Word. His Word lives within. He lives to exalt us.

Chapter III

Tea with Jesus

Wounded soul, enter My rest.
Wounded soul, become a house guest.

Friend of God

God is our husband, Father and our friend.

How is it possible that God can be all three to us? Oh, Sheri, I am intertwined and so much in love with you, that there is no way I can separate myself, even though you have a variety of needs. My character is like a rope of threads all different colors that wraps anywhere I send it.

One of the most exciting things about sending Jesus to earth to bring you Salvation, is that I was able to interject with the Holy Spirit. Before he came, the Holy Spirit did not live in every one that calls out to him. I only gave my Spirit to who I willed. Not, that you can will my Spirit to come into yourself, but, now that Jesus has paved the way, my Spirit comes into anyone who asks. It was given as a free gift as part of the package for Salvation.

Salvation brought new birth; spiritual regeneration where those who are dead can become alive through the joining with the blood sacrifice of Jesus Christ. For, you are dead in your sins without being born again.

There is no way for you to deal with your own sin. You cannot pay the price, and not die. My judgment falls on sin. It is part of My character. I cannot change. And, heaven is a place where My presence dwells, so it is a holy place. There is no room for sin there because it is My house. I don't tolerate evil at My house.

And, I gave you an opportunity to not tolerate sin at your house, as well, by allowing you to tag onto the train of Jesus. It is like He is a railroad train that runs along the track of My righteousness. I put a hook on the back that is just the right size for you to hook your caboose to. And, just like a train, you cannot hook to the train without getting onto the rails of the track. Your car has to fit the track to be able to go there. The rails on Jesus' track are My righteousness. I need to have you without sin, so you can stay on the track. When you are righteous, then, you can hook onto the caboose and go up and down My hills and into My Heavenly Kingdom.

The problem is that you are not righteous on your own. So, again I have provided help. You can go into the repair shop and get fitted for the rails. At my repair shop, I will fit you with what you need. That is all there is to it. You only need to be willing to be fitted for My track.

I have a lot of room at the repair shop and a team standing by. But, you need to be willing to turn your car over to Me for a while. It is like leaving the car at the auto shop for repairs. You need to leave yourself at My repair shop for a while. Just bring your old car in, set it in My garage, and turn over the keys to Me. I have a whole retrofit program in place to bring you up to speed with all the other cabooses.

And, when you turn over the keys to Me, leave them there. For, you won't need them any more. I will drive for you. Just come to me, come to the cross of Jesus, claim His forgiveness for your sin, and pick up your holiness. I will fit your car with My holiness. You let go, I give.

People get that part mixed up. It is not about you giving your heart to Me, it's about Me giving My heart to you. It's just that when your heart is full of yourself, there is no room for Me. So, your job is to let your heart go. Give as much of yourself to Me as possible. I will not disappoint you, I promise. For, when you leave yourself at My repair shop and I fit you with My purity and holiness, then I will set you on the track that you were meant to be on. Then, the fun will start.

You can go as fast as you want, when you are on the track I have prepared for you. I will be your guide to help you keep between the rails of My provision. As you see into the future by faith through prayer, I will become bigger and bigger in your vision. My kingdom will come into view, just over the bend. That is it! You sail into My Kingdom on the rails of My righteousness following the plans I have set for you.

And, I don't leave you. I have parallel tracks right next to you. My train runs along side as fast as you go. We keep pace with one another. We can look into the windows and chat across the cars.

Luke 7.34, 11.5, 12.4, 14.10-12, 15.6-29, John 3.29, 15.13-15.

Jesus is our Friend

I had no friends until I learned what this meant. I had acquaintances: Friendly people in my life for a specific purpose. Time limited relationships based on mutual need. My Jesus friend is neither. Now, I have learned to be a forever, friend. And, my cup is spilling over to others. Because, we are all eternal.

Why couldn't I have a friend in you, forever? Let's be friends. Faithful, tested, time warn, eternal buddies. Pals, compadres. Allow Me an entrance to see the beauty within your soul. Open your window to Mine. I will open mine and we can chat across the flowers. You from your house, and Me from mine.

When we ask Jesus to forgive us through His blood, There is a window to our soul opened. Next, we need to invite the cool breeze of the Holy Spirit to enter. For, He is the wind that carries the voice of God into our house. He carries it like a red ribbon in the beak of a blue bird. He will bring that streamer. He ties the bow.

Forms the knot of the covenant between us and God. Like the rainbow? He gives demonstrations of his covenant. The Holy Spirit is a fulfillment of a covenant. He is the present wrapped by a bow, a deal between the Father, the Son, and the Holy Spirit. We open the window Of our heart to receive the fulfillment of the covenant; the Gift.

Prince of Awakening

Oh dawn of the morning come to us.

Prince of awakening, awaken our hearts to sing of Your new mercy, today.

You are the dawn of our awakening.

Without you mercy and grace, we would remain in darkness, pain and despair.

Become in us, the new life, we need.

We pray, Oh, Lord Jesus Christ, renew our hearts to Your love.

Conference Call

The Combination to unlock the bondages of the enemy is love. It is God's phone number. Like numbers on a telephone, you can call on His love again and again. He is on the other side of the line any time, day or night. It is His Personal back office line. We experience that love when we share it with others. A conference call.

Open Appointment

The office is open 24 hours. You can come without an appointment. Enter through the stone door. The rock has been rolled away. Come to see the King. It's always different for the children of the Senior Executive.

Adopted One

E're you lost me, I was His. E're you found me. Now I'm Yours. Forever I will stay bound by a pledge eternal covenant. Father to son, dad to His kid Arise, O adopted one And pick up your certificate.

Job Evaluation

Measure your success by Me. You don't have to wait until you get to heaven to know if you did a good job. Just ask now. As you take your voice lessons, don't be afraid to ask the instructor, once in a while, For feed back. Ask Him how you sound.

My November Job Evaluation

Can I have a job evaluation, Lord? Help me out here. You are like a ball found under a blackberry bush. How? The kids threw it out of bounds and you have retrieved it. There were stickers grown over it. The seasons had passed and I was truly worried that no one would go looking in that place. But you did. Under that bush. You have torn up your arms going straight into the place that was the most treacherous. Through the thorny bushes where others did not want to get injured. You came on in. And, you were not gentle. The problem is that you prayed in so much hunger, that you would go straight through the mountain to get to the answer. I am a mountain of rock. And you thought there had to be some way to get to Me. You would have taken a chisel and a hammer and pecked away at the rock your whole life. And, you would have done it. With each hammer full of rock, you would know that you were closer to the answer. But, I opened the door. In a place within the rock you didn't know existed. Thanks. It was an abandoned well. Amen. Thanks for the evaluation, Lord. I love you.

Frosted Wheat

Frosted wheat is an example of how we sometimes sugar coat things in an attempt to get the children to eat what is good for them. The sweetness of God is baked within His word. We do not need to add to it. It comes with baked in goodness.

Between Meal Snacks

An apple and a chocolate bar.
Between meal snacks.
Fruit and sweetness always available from the one we love.
O Holy Spirit pack a sack of snacks for in between.

Chocolates

There is dark delight and light delight.
Like light and dark chocolate.
God brings His sweetness day and night.

Apple

Bite what is in your hand. **It's an apple.**

There is an interaction between the fruits of the Holy Spirit, what we need to take in, and what we hold. What we hold is what we need to work from. Sometimes we think that we need to go outside of our relationship with God to find Him. That is not so. He is found within what He has already provided. Not in a new sermon, a new song, a new verse. Everything we need to have a complete relationship with Him has already been given through Jesus.

The dream says, "Look at what I have already given to you. Focus on that."

It is an apple. We are the apple of God's eye, His beloved ones, therefore, He gives us the fruits of the Holy Spirit. It is because of the relationship with Him as His child, that He gives us the inheritance within the Spiritual Kingdom. He is calling us to take a bite into that which He has given.

It is a special place in the center of the heart that where we will find the fullness of the fruit. We have been given fruits from the tree of life containing the seeds of eternal life. The seeds give life to the body of Christ. The fruits of the Holy Spirit need to be bit into to release what is inside. Just as we eat away at the flesh of an apple to get to the seeds, we need to allow our flesh to be eaten away by his refining process to get to His seeds.

We must get our own flesh out of the way, to see the direction of the voice of the Holy Spirit. It is His voice that gives us insight to get to the core of the issues that we are facing. He has made a provision for us to have a relationship with Him, our core to His. It is the center of His heart connecting to the center of ours. Heart to heart. The flesh has no part of the relationship with God. We give ourselves completely over to His purposes to get to the seeds of His intension for us.

We need to learn how to relate to God apart from others. He has given each of us all we need to be satisfied within the center of our soul.

The second message of the dream is that the word of God is found within the fruit. When we open the fruit that He has given us, we will find His Word.

He has given each of us gifts. These gifts need to be opened to get to what is inside. The gift needs to be unwrapped, like biting into an apple, to release the flavor. The message of God needs to be released by opening the fruit. When we open up to Him, the flesh is displayed, but do not dismay, He also has a message for us within that place. The messages of God are hidden within the fruit. Wisdom, knowledge, understanding, counsel, might, presence and fear of the Lord are the seven Spirits of God which are released through biting into the fruit that He has put into our hand.

Each time we ask Him for the answer to a question, and we open ourselves up to receive the answer, we have put aside our flesh, and listen to Him. As we do, He moves us, with the fruits of his Holy Spirit using the gifts of the Holy Spirit, and tells us the answer. He reveals to us through His wisdom, and counsel, the answer. We bite into what is in our hand.

Psalms 17. 8, Pr 7.2, Isaiah 11, Colossians 2.9-15.

God Wakes Us

You would not get up unless I woke you.
I will be your uprising.

Comfort Food

Cream soup is comfort food because we eat it on a dreary day when it's rainy outside. We snuggle by the warmth of a toasty fire with our mom and float oyster crackers in the bowl making shapes while we eat our way to the bottom of the bowl. The crackers swim by like little fish in our aquarium. Why do they call it comfort food? Because, it provides warmth from within that permeates outwards. When we drink the warm milk of the word, we are like kittens seeking a snack. The warm milk makes us snuggly inside. Then, as we sit in His presence by the fire, He warms us inside and out; all around He snuggles us. That's why they call it comfort food. He is our comfort.

Eye, Ear, and Face to Face with God

Eye to eye, ear to ear, face to face.

God wants us to see eye to Him. He came to earth to be able to see things our way. He took on human form to be able to think like a human. He had physical eyes to be able to see from our vantage point. He knows how we feel as we walk around on the earth. We can share all of ourselves with Him, because He understands.

Even though He is the God of the universe, He still understands what it is to be a human. He wants us to see eye to eye with Him. We need to set our eye level with His eyes. When we look into His eyes, we will see ourselves as we truly are and we will see Him as He is. We will understand Him when He shows us His vision, His view of things.

He wants us to hear Him and He wants to hear us. He is a verbal kind of a Guy. He wants us to communicate with Him day and night. He loves us intensely and wants us always to reach out with our heart to speak to Him about everything. He hears every thought of our mind and heart. Nothing escapes His ears. He hears the prayers of our heart.

He also, wants us to hear the prayers of His heart. He speaks day and night, as well. He speaks to us in our spirit, in visions and in voice in the daytime. At night, He speaks in dreams. And, on rare occasions, He will speak with His voice.

I have heard them all. Sometimes, it is difficult to tell whether or not I hear His voice with my ears or with my spirit, because it comes to me so loudly. At one time I asked God to turn up the volume so I could hear Him better.

He said to me, "Sheri, I do not change. You are asking Me to change. What you need to do is to turn down your own noise. The television, the radio, the incessant telephone calls, and, most of all, your own thoughts that build your own dreams. Let go of these, and seek Me in the place of quietness within your heart."

We need to practice turning down the 'ambient' noise in our lives so that we can hear God better. He is talking to us all of the time, but often, we can't hear Him because there is too much other noise and it is drowning Him out as His voice comes to us.

God, also, wants to come to us, face to face. He wants us to find that place where He is. For each of us, it is a different and special place. He has prepared times of close encounters with Him. We need to see with His vision where He is, listen for His voice, then follow the sound of His voice to go to Him. He is like a Father calling out to His children. When we turn off the noise in our lives and listen to His call, then we will be able to follow His voice to Him.

He is always at the end of His voice. Sometimes, we need to travel further to see His face, but it is always there, just like a Father's face is always at the end of his voice. Our God is a faithful God who is waiting with open arms extended to us, ready to embrace us with His tenderness.

His Buds

Over and above, around and through,
I love you. Do you, too?
Let's get together like buds on a cherry tree.
You bloom and I will supply the fragrance.

Giver of Dreams

You can have what you dream of. Ask.
From the Heaven Sent, Already Risen, Savior.
He is waiting. Ask.

Scents of God

To see, to hear, to smell, to touch. All senses given to us from our Holy Redeemer to see His face, hear His voice, catch wisps of His cologne and reach out into the heavenly place where He dwells. These golden opportunities are ours.

Since He sent His Son, it's summer time. Smell the blooms. When we sense Him, we can bloom. When we see Him, we can dance. When we Hear Him, we can sing. If we smell him, then He's very close because God has no odor but Himself.

He's as clean as the driven snow. What does snow smell like. I'm not sure. But, I know what it tastes like.

I'm not sure if I've smelled God, but I know for sure that I have tasted of Him. And, He tastes awesome. His and mine are similar. We like the same things. Love, peace, joy, freedom from sin, deliverance, delight. And we both like good music.

We love to sing together, and to have the sense to smell Him now.

Crocodile Tears

Crocodile tears roll down
My face as once more you
Touch my heart with Your love.
For, when you break my stony heart,
water comes out. Salty, like sea water.
For, now I see who I really am. And, I see, to,
how once again, I need you And, as I am touched,
not merely by my unfaithfulness, but Yours continuing.
For, it doesn't seem to matter where I stop being faithful,
You pick up where I leave off.
And, sometimes, it's pretty early in the trail, I sit down. But,
You come along and finish the hike. You pick up my water
bottle and walk where I should have gone. Then, You thank
me for permitting You to do it. All I did was sit down,
tired, and discouraged and You picked up where
I left off. All I did was cry out
to You. Yet,
You
are
the first to say, 'thank you.'
So,
once
again,
I am
overwhelmed
By Your love which I
could never think to match.
But, still, Lord,
I say, 'Thank You' back. Because,
even it is belated, I know You appreciate it.
So, 'thank you', Lord for taking my place on that trail
that I found too hard. Please give me endurance for next time.

Pray Bo Who

Crying prayer is not necessarily sad. It is prayer filled
with emotion. Intense feelings well up from within and
spill over the cheeks. Is it happy? Not necessarily. It
is intense, pulsating emotion in its truest form. The
love of God. If you are happy to find the love, it
is one of exuberance. If you have sin to deal with,
it is one of remorse. It is always a cleaning party.
Like spring cleaning, He shows us the sin; the
clothes we should no longer wear, and we
get rid of them. Toss them out. Then His
love floods that place where sin lived.
Like old clothes thrown out,
He comes with a new
Wardrobe of His
righteous
garments
to clothe us with.
And, it's overwhelming.
The more we clean out,
the more we fill up. That
the scripture is true.
He who is forgiven
much, loves
much.
How, I love
to toss old clothes
from my walk in closet while in
prayer. Old sins thrown
in a heap at the
foot of the
cross.
Then, ask for new ones.
It's very intense and overwhelming.
But, my goal is to go to a deeper love each
time. Hopefully, by the time, I reach glory, I won't
have too many of my old clothes left to exchange.

Face to Face with Issues

When we run into personal issues that need cleansing, it depends on how urgent our need is as to how far we get off the trail. If we have an intense relationship with God, then we will be urgent to get back into that fellowship with Him. We won't stay off the trail long. Often, others won't even notice that we are off the trail. We may go just to the side and deal with the issues between our Lord and us. We need to come face to face with Him and face to face with the issue at the same time.

Window of our Heart

Then, I saw the mountain off in the distance. It had been there all the time, just I had never looked out the window. Five years I spent in that room looking out the window. But, why had I never seen that mountain until today? Because we only see what we are looking for. We hear activity in the street, and we look. We wonder what the weather is doing, so we look at the sunrise. We notice movement, and our eyes are drawn to it with a question. It is like we look out the window to put the question mark at the end of the sentence. If we don't look out the window, we still question without resolving, even the question. The Holy Spirit is this way. We wonder about Him, about the things they are saying. The miracles, the speaking in strange voices, the power flow.

We wonder. But, we must look out the window for it to be turned into a question that has a mark at the end of it. Our thoughts need to move from the place of wondering about what others are saying, like hearing noise out the window, to looking for ourselves. Each of us has the ability to look out the window of our heart and ask God questions. The window to see God is the same size for all of us. Oh, we see those who say they 'hear from God' all the time. And, we think that, surely, they must have a picture window. We, reason, that God has only given us a fogged bathroom window. But, that is not true. He does not favor His children, He loves them all the same. It's just that there are kids that come to Him more often and crawl up on His lap, and ask Him questions. Then, they wait for Him to answer. Then, there are other kids who ask questions of Him while they are running out the back door to do their own thing. So, you can see, from a father's perspective, that He loves the ones that come to Him, lean on Him and show caring. Because, they are the ones that He has a chance to demonstrate His love to. You see, He wants to show His love to us. We need to let Him. We cut him off, though. We close the blinds and turn the television on. We blast our brain with loud music that sings of other lovers. We cloud our thinking with romance that was never meant to be.

We venture into fights between people who never should be fighting. And, we try to forget about the window. The window of our heart to see God. But, today, it turned the blinds. I opened them in a way that I never have before since I bought this house five years ago. And I saw them. The mountains afar off. They were beautiful with the sun reflecting against the rock slide. And, I noticed things I had never seen before.

Our Conquest Against Sin

Lust, agony, resentment, torment. We lust for what we don't have. We agonize over plans we want to happen. We torment our Soul for unfulfilled expectations. Alexander the Great, mighty conqueror of old. Lead a successful conquest through many countries to become his own desires. Did he become himself? No, He was himself when he was born and he was The same himself when He died. Naked he came and naked he left. Lust, agony, resentment, torment of his soul. Were those on list of kingdoms to conquer? Or, did he never, take his army there? I hope so, but I don't think so. Because, no matter how might of an army we build here on earth, we will never conquer our own sinful nature. Only one Conquesta led His army to absolute total victory. Jesus and Me. The one man R Me. Join today.

Others Seedlings

The Dream:

My neighbor shows me some seedlings. I'm not sure whether or not she is going to give them to me. I don't think that they will grow here anyway. So, I opt to go to the store myself and get my own.

Interpretation:

God wants us to go to His storehouse to get our own seeds. He will grow his word in us. The seeds that God gives to us are individual. They grow in our environment, our climate and in our yard. God gives seed specific to certain climates and individuals.

For me, He is able to teach me extensively about hearts and his body because I am a nurse who works with sick hearts all the time. I see how man tries to heal them from the outside, inward. There is a lot of scaring and pain. Through my life and environment, God has developed a specific training program. It fits me. It is mine. He has shown me that often we cause pain in other areas of the body while we try to fix the heart. He talks to me in specific ways because of who I am and where I live.

He has a seed packet for all to be grown in the environment that they are living within. He knows their needs and the soil that they have in their yards. We need to ask Him to give us the seeds that are supposed to grow within our yard. Others will try to give us their seed packet, but it doesn't work within our climate.

Just like there are many climates and soils in the world, there are many people living in those places. God knows the soils. He made them. And, He knows us. He has provided a seed packet specifically designed for our soil. We need to consult the grower, and ask for ours. It's free.

Father, please give us your seed packet for our lives. Give us the word into our heart specifically fitted to us. We are frustrated using others seeds. Help us, Please, Dear Lord.

Candy Wrappers

The wrappers that hold the candy are the best part. We are the wrappers that hold the sweetness of God within our heart. It's the part where we wrap ourselves around Him and He lives within. When we share our life with others through the gifts of the Holy Spirit, we become like chocolates to be shared with the Children of God. A box of chocolates has the sweets, the wrappers, the box and the bow. The sweetness of the Holy Spirit is what fills us. We wrap around His filling with our lives. He boxes us to be in a place where He can hand us to others. There is always a bow around the outside. We are marked by a covenant of His love and forgiveness every time we share the sweetness of the Holy Spirit with others.

Tight Hold

Help me remember, O Lord, the changes that you are making in me are not for your benefit, but mine. I am like the diamond in Your hand. You press me to clarify me. When it seems I am in a cave, it is merely Your hand closing around me once again to hold me tighter.

Fields of Worship

All I did, Lord, was take the key you put in my pocket, go
to the middle of the field you gave me, extend my hand
and open it. And, I didn't move. I stayed there,
hands extended, arms open, rain and shine. Five
years. It is only Your grace that makes
me walk.
I have boxed fields of love
waiting to be delivered to you.
Ask. I will give you your inheritance.
The field. It will be work, but I will provide
the sun, and the rain. I will make you to be wealthy
and happy. The fields of My love are all kinds of shapes
and colors. Some are for the sheep to graze on. Some are
to help them when they think their put out to pasture.
Some are birthing stalls where dreams are birthed.
There you become like a momma to them. I send
Full grown, fat with baby, sheep, and you help
move them into their vision. That is a momma.
Then, there are the wheat fields. Those who
Sow the word for others to chew on.
Preachers and teachers and sharers
of good news. Maybe, you
are a tulip field.
One meant to display my bulbs, to bring light.
Revelation and understanding.
It could
be you
offer
seasonal crops.
Summer fruits and vegetables.
A word in season, at just the right time.
By the grace that I offer, ask. I am waiting
to answer. I have Your inheritance in my hand.

Where is the Core?

In most of the things money can buy, its changed. Honor is not valued as it should be. Intimacy has been neglected. Programs have replaced relationships. There is no longer an expectancy of security with commitment. As the dependency on his Holy Spirit has been bled from our lives, our character has been eroded. Like a bar of soap in the shower. It has been eaten away by the enemy pounding at us in ways we are not prepared to handle. Cleaver tactics full of deceptive manipulation meant to control God's children have been used skillfully by Satan.

He has stunted our growth. He has tainted our weed and feed causing us to be unproductive. We are barren. We produce sterile apples that have no seed because the core is messed up. It all goes back to the core. We have been deluded to think that love and physical demonstration are equal.

If someone does not show us that they love us, then it is not so. This limits our thinking to the here and now. Temporal. God is kicked out of the picture. Like a television set, we have torn out some of the picture tubes, so our picture is not complete. We have problems with our ability to receive his signals because our equipment has been damaged. So, our picture of his love is fuzzy.

The problem is that we are unbalanced. There is too many lines going horizontal and not enough going vertical. We have lost our ability to focus. It is like when we study for a career, we must focus on the new subject to learn things that have been previously unfamiliar to us. It does not really matter how hard the subject is, if we are interested in it. When we focus on it, we begin to grasp it. Before long, we find that we have entered a new field and learned things we didn't know before.

It's like that with God. Think of him as a new field. In fact, he is in a field that is out of this world. He is in a field of His own. Now, in order for us to learn about Him, we must focus our attention in the direction of the subject.

We try. We read the Bible and pray. We memorize Scripture, attend Bible studies and Church. We go to Bible school. But, we are unbalanced because we have not learned responsive prayer.

What we are missing is openness with God. Unadulterated truth. He is the way, the truth and the life. We have separated our thinking. We want the way and we seek eternal life and healing for today, yet we have not come to Him to learn the truth.

When we open our heart to Him and ask Him to reveal His truth, we need to stop and stay; pause for His answer. We have gotten so used to one way prayer, that we don't even allow for the pause after our own words.

Oh, people! Be encouraged to put a pause into your prayer. For, that is His voice you drown out with your own. That is the core, the seed that He means to grow in your heart to help you to understand Him.

Then, our television will have the vertical lines, as well, and the picture of who He is, and who we are will become more clear.

Opacity

The clarity determines the depth of the message
I am   able to
send through   the individual.
One that is open to me.
True
to
Their
own heart,
And true to others. Opaque.

Chapter IV

Praise

The children have taught me how to release the restraint that was never supposed to be there in the first place.

Jesus' Boat

Dream:

I go to the sea. There's a place where people are to stand together. It looks like a choir stand. The sea is behind and it faces the beach. The benches are wavy. There are several elevations where people can stand. It would be a large choir. The middle is finished, but the sides are not done yet. The people would stand there together and do the wave as they look like a wave.

I go to a house and talk with Jesus. He dies. I spend the night kneeling at his bedside. In the morning it is light. Now, I am asked to return His boat. I am not sure how to get there, but I start out. He borrowed it and I need to bring it back to the people.

Interpretation:

God is building a choir, one that will praise Him at the sea. He wants us to see him as He really is. Then, we will stand side by side and wave, even as we stand still.

When we move, there will be a large movement of air. The air flows through His people in waves. God is starting the book from the middle and working outward. I am building a choir stand; a place for the birds to sing. It is a place for people to stand and sing to, Him, together.

I see how He has died to bring us the light. My image of Him died

83

which allowed Him to give light to a new image. It brought back the stance where He can preach to them, Himself.

In the dream, I am asked to bring His boat back. He sees it as a rowboat. I have seen it, in a huge vision in the desert as I hiked, as an aircraft carrier. He wants His carrier to return to His people from whom it was taken. God wants to bring whatever we need. It will come as we see Him as He really is and come to Him for as our need meter.

In the dream, I don't get in the boat. I walk on water to bring it. The boat is not mine. The Father has provided, through the death of Jesus, a boat for each of us. It is His provision to provide everything we need to meet Him by faith. We must learn how to walk on the water to reach the boat, as Peter did, in the New Testament. We need to learn to answer Jesus' voice and walk toward it in faith.

In the dream, I am told that Jesus borrowed it. If we look at his life here on the earth, He used faith to walk toward the voice of God and fulfill the mission He was called to do. We are now called to use the same faith that He had, to fulfill the visions of his Father.

In the dream the boat is tied to the beach by a long chain. It is rusty with age.

His words are, "Don't forget the chain. Don't just talk around it. The blood needs to be in the book. When you got there, I carried you. Teach them how. Remember the steps? The pressure of God? By infusion. The Blood.

The book needs to be pushable from unbelief into reality. By faith.

Remember the steps. Allow yourself to feel the pain. The pain of separation from the One who created you. Go to the desert and see how dry it is. Even when it rains, it develops into a flash flood that does not profit the plants that grow there. It is dry, hot, dusty. There's a fine red silt that sticks to your socks and shoes. It burns your eyes. There is no water except what you bring. What you carry.

I went to the desert outside of Las Vegas. Then, I talked to Him. He was the only one there. Desolation and hunger is what I felt. My heart had been hardened by sin. I had built a garden on that rock. It was tender moss and delicate flowers that I showed to others.

Then, I turned the rock over and grew some on the other side. But when I turned it over, the moss on the bottom died. Each time I turned the rock of my heart over, a piece of me died. I was alive but dead.

Living a lie, attempting to convince myself it was true.

Where was truth? I could not face it. It was too brutal. It would destroy me; tear me to shreds, dismantle my personality. I had tried therapy. I spent $5000 going to someone with a fake name who charged me for advice that caused me to leave my husband. This left my children without a father. It only brought more ruin to my family. I had shared me lies with them to no profit. I did not find God there...because he wasn't. He does not live in the places where we try to make excuses for going our own direction. He stands in the place where we left Him, and sobs for us.

I followed my own ideas of who God was. I built an image of what Jesus had done for me. Then, I paid tribute to it. I sacrificed to my golden calf. I set it high on a pedestal and encouraged those around me to serve it. But, it was not true, because it was an image that I built myself.

I had taken all of the ideas that I held precious, all of my precious gold jewelry, and formed a beast. It never gave me anything back. It was a cow that gives no milk.

It was barren, just like the desert. It only stood in my path, preventing me from going the direction that I was supposed to go. My $5000 had bought me an expensive statue. So, I fell down and worshiped that beast.

You see, you have to fall down before you worship. When you are outside of the place where God intended you to be, then there is a lot of tripping and falling. Then, when you trip, you think that you are out of line with God, so you give. You give to a charity or Church basket. You try to spend more time with someone that you really hate. You press yourself into service, for what you have come to worship.

But, that golden calf will give no milk. He can't. He will only reflect whatever you have made him out of. So, I came to the point where I was at the end of the rope dangling over the fire. I could feel the flames lapping at my legs, ready to consume everything that I had done in my life because none of it was worth anything.

How did I get here? God told me to tell you. He carried me. I let go of the rope and fell into the fire. I turned myself over to His mercy. I decided that it was either true, or not. And, I pushed Him. I pushed God for the answer.

I stopped hiding my desolate heart from myself. I was the golden cow. I had glazed over what needed to be melted down to make the jewelry He wanted me to wear.

I cried out with everything I had. And I still do. I cry to my creator for His Mercy is Everlasting and He does not withhold His love to us. Then, I put the other distractions aside. I stepped out of all of the teaching that I had been given. I turned the television and the radio off. I quit reading the newspaper. And, I slowly turned my face toward Him.

It was very painful, as His light exposed the decay in my life. I would turn a little at a time, as much as I could bear. The light is so bright that it hurts the heart.

But, just like a runner training for a match, each time I would push. Push a little further in. Into the light that exposed the pain that I had caused myself and my family. That heart was so full of dark secrets of decay that I could see snakes come out of the holes like eels live in the shell of the coral reef. I was a coral reef, bones where life used to live. And the enemy had taken up comfortable residence in that place.

The light of God is like a fiber optic instrument. The channel of His light bends. The light does not bend. The channel of light bends in the hand of the Great Physician. He brings to light the things hidden since the beginning of time so that He can bring us to Himself and heal us.

So, I did nothing but voice my need to my Creator. I needed an infusion of blood. A transfusion with the blood of the Lamb. To be made new. Afresh. I sought to live, not merely be alive. To walk, not merely stand. I could envision myself before the throne of Jesus after I died.

I wanted to take care of the sin issue here on earth, so that when I got there, I could run into his arms. I didn't want to be one of those people who fall at this feet out of grief for what I had done and not done while here on earth. I wanted no regret; to come to His face without regret.

But how? I threw down my tools. Everything I had. I was alone. No other person came with me. Just me and God. And I threw abandonment to the wind. I brought my abandonment to Him and unleashed it.

Then, I prayed. I prayed Scripture. Verses, chapters, books. Every time I prayed for someone else, what ever I prayed for them, I also, prayed for myself. I sought His blessing in my life. I came abandoned and left my arms open waiting for Him to show up.

And I kept coming back. Little by little abandonment gave way to filling. The filling gave way to filled. The filled became overflow. Then, the top blew off the volcano. Lava spewed down to the sea.

I dared to believe the dreams were from Him. Then, I took a chance that the visions might be true also. Never once has He disappointed me. They have all been true. It is I that have not always been true to them.

He is a faithful tennis player. He lobs the ball into my court play after play to keep the score love, love. It is me that runs out of bounds into the bushes. I use the back hand when I should use the forward swing. I worry that my arm will not be strong enough, but I forget that it is Him that empowers even my arm to return the volley to Him.

Then, He started to talk. It is not that He started to talk for the first time. It is that I started to understand what He was saying. I realized that He had been talking all along, but I never heard Him.

The voice of God comes to the heart, not the mind. He speaks to us as a child because that is what we are. He speaks to the heart, then, we must transfer the information to our mind to understand it. The transformation needs to be pure, unabridged, innocent, and tender like a small child responds to their parent.

It is like, when I was a child, asleep and my mother would gently come into my room and wake me. She would whisper. It would sink into my subconscious ears first, then work its way up to my conscious, until I woke up. Jesus comes that way. He whispers into our heart, then, it passes through to our subconscious. If there are blocks, then it will not pass through. We will not hear His voice.

If you want to hear God, clear out the blocks. Get rid of the dead wood in your life. Gather it up and burn it. It is the season to burn. In Washington, where I was raised, there are a lot of trees. To clear the land, they log the trees, pull the stumps, then, when it is burning season, they burn the stumps. We are logging the trees, confessing our sin, but we are not burning the stumps.

We are not allowing the healing power of the Holy Spirit to infiltrate us and pull up the stumps. They have to be pulled up before they can be burned. This means visiting those painful experiences in our lives and opening ourselves up to receive his healing. It hurts, I know. But little, by little, the land will be cleared and make way to plant new growth. He wants to make us new. He wants to make new growth on our lot.

You can always push God. He will do a whole lot of clearing if you are ready for it. I believe He has an assignment held in His hand for each of us. It is up to us how fast we want to get to that place where we can do it.

Noah took his sweet time building the Ark. He could have done it much faster, but he didn't. He was a carpenter, yet it took him 100 years to build a single boat. I think he stalled. I got here in four years. I pushed. I pushed, and He pushed back. He loves to be pushed. Did you *know that you can change the mind of God? It's the only thing about Him that changes. Ask Moses.*

Why We Praise God

There is confusion about the word praise. Praise is laud to Me for who I am. I have created you, yet you have turned from Me. I didn't stop reproducing your cells, did I? I didn't automatically allow Satan to come in to ruin your family, Take your stuff and tear you apart. It's frustrating to Me when I, as the artist, have created you. And yet, you refuse to recognize it. How do you think you got here? And, you presume upon the food that I provide.

If there was no rain, no river, no fertile valley, there would be no crops. You presume upon the meat, as well. Who tells the animals when to mate, so they will reproduce after their kind? And, do you think that they automatically all end up reproducing their cells day after day by happenstance?

What about the days, the seasons, the tides, the winds? How do they happen? And, your ability to think, to move,to walk, to love others. Where does this come from? Me. You didn't fall out of the sky. You were born from two single cells, hand grown by My supervision within your mother's womb. I planned the color of your eyes, your hair and your personality. And, I continue to sustain you. I am God. All power flows from Me. Satan has no power, except what he has received from Me. Remember, the gifts and the calling are irrevocable. I don't change My word once I send it out. He was created and given an ability to know how to draw power from Me.

And, so he continues. You do to. You rise up in the morning, put on your socks and go to work without a thought about how your heart keeps beating. You don't pause and wonder why you continue to breath. You presume upon My grace. For that is what it is. My grace. So, should it be strange that I would call you to recognize Me for who I am?

But, yet I did not stop there. It would seem enough for Me to continue to sustain you, But, I have done more than that. I have inclined Myself to become intimately involved in your life. I want to become your friend. There is a sin problem.

I am a holy fire. I can't help it. It is My personality. So, to be able to be your friend, I had to protect you from the fire. So, I gave you a fire retardant suit, so you can come to My world, yet not die. You must put the suit on, to withstand the hot temperatures. The heat is My love. It burns with passion over you, My children. *But, for some, they don't really catch on for a while. They are too afraid to enter the flame. Jesus is Me. Hello. I have given Myself to you, so that you can be able to come be with Me. I took on a form that you know, I became* a man.

Then, I dealt with the sin issue, once and for all. I was the perfect Sacrifice, because I am perfect. You see, I was the only one who could do it, because there is only one perfect God. It's not that I enjoy suffering, but the Sacrifice had to be very specific to meet all of the requirements needed. I figured that if I was going to give My life in the human form, then I would go for the gold. And I did.

By Jesus' death, there are hundreds of benefits given to you is because the Sacrifice was perfect, as My love is perfect for you. It's all about the love, anyway. The word, I created to show My love. Then, the animals I created, to show My love.

Then, you, I created to show My love. You are the crown of My creation. For, it is you that has a spirit able to commune with Mine on a spiritual level. And I want it to do that. When we commune, we interact spirit to Spirit, then your spirit reaches out to Mine and Mine to yours. You put on the Jesus Fireproof Suit and walk into the fire of My love, and we talk. It is there that you, not *only have knowledge of who I am, but come to know Me.*

It is when you come to know Me, that your spirit will praise. It will reach out in praise to Me because there will be an awakening to understand some of how I uphold the universe by My power. And you will become grateful. It is a good thing. Not that I have deliberately contended for your gratefulness, for I am God, I do not need anything, yet, it warms my heart. Oh, now you have come to know that My heart can be warmed. And, you have become like Me, in that you have a fire. It was started by Me, sustained by Me, but comes from your spirit. And as it flows from your spirit to Mine, I become warmed by your love.

Cool, hua? That is the result of praise. Why would I not want to praise My God?

Heart Praise

God is looking for those who desire to worship Him in spirit and truth from their heart. Where have we gone? We have been given a plastic version of worship. We have come to believe that worship is what we do on Sunday morning.

But, God reminds us that worship is when He comes into our heart in such a way that His Spirit flows through our entire being to make our hearts sing to Him in a way, only we can. It is personal. It has eternal tones that display things that we think have been lost long ago. He is risen. He is alive to live within us to help us.

I pray Holy Spirit, May our lives bring praise to you.

Reaching to God

Eternal, immortal God, I lift my soul to you. As high as I can. Which is actually probably only about four feet from earth. I guess, if I stretch or get on a ladder, I could lift it about 20 feet. With the help of man made structures, together, we could lift it a mile into the air. But, who wants to do that? All the riches are found on the floor kneeling at your feet. So, I'll just stay put and ask You to come to me. Fly To me, O wings of the Dove. Merge my spirit With yours.

Give me colorful iridescent wings like the angels that make hawks jealous. Oh, Father, I need wings that have enough span to, not merely lift me, but those I pray for. Because, I have a lot of needs I want to bring to you. Some are very big. Maybe rather than giving me wings, just swoop down and let me hold onto yours. Because, I've heard that you can lift anything by Your power alone. Let it be so, my Lord!

A Singing Soul

One who sings alone to the one she loves. The thing with a singing soul is that Others are eager to listen in because it is so rare. There are rules with singing souls. They have to be willing to share. Not all the time-There are times that you pig God: You don't share Him with anyone. Oh, you can feel others nudging in to intrude, but, you cherish this time and shun them. They can go find their own. He is yours. Like a husband. All yours.

Rebuke of a Demon

Dream:

A very scary demon comes to me. It is so real, I am not sure it is a dream. At first, I can only whisper Jesus' name.

The demon backs up and I sing a praise song to God.

Then, I say, "Holy, Holy, Holy."

He comes back into my face, attempting to scare me.

Then, I say, "I rebuke you in the name of the Lord Jesus Christ."

And the demon leaves.

In between the whole time, I am speaking in tongues.

Interpretation:

I woke up knowing he was here. So, I asked God about it. Here is what He said:

Sheri, you know power over the enemy is in the name of Jesus. He can never prevent you from calling out to Me. That is something I have never authorized him to be able to do. But, the matrix of the dream gives a combination for complete victory. Follow it.

First, claim Jesus as your Savior.

Give praise to God, for His Salvation is through His love.

Claim His holiness for yourself through the blood of Jesus Christ. His holiness becomes yours, as you are one of His adopted children. Put on His holy robe of righteousness.

The demonic powers only can scare. They have no authority to touch unless it is given.

My angels will protect you from them. What do you think they are there for? Remember, however, you don't send angels, I do. They are sent from My throne to help you, not roaming around the earth to do as you beckon.

Then, as you are covered under the provision of the holiness of God through the blood of Jesus, assume your authority as a child of God. Rebuke it.

Reprove: to call the demon to the carpet. When you reprove him, you remind him who is in charge. You tell him the truth; that God is in charge and the battle has been won already by Jesus' blood. You reprove the facts, and disprove the theory of deceit of the enemy. Display the truth.

For, truth slits the throat of the enemy. So, the combination is to know the truth and speak it. Declare it in the presence of the demon.

Take up your cross and follow Jesus. For, when you take up the cross, you bury sin and claim victory. Each time you bury sin, you take away excuses of the enemy to point his finger and accuse you of wrong. When he accuses you, he gains advantage.

If you simply say that you are a sinner, it saves time. Humility is a vital key, up front. For when you claim you are a sinner and ask for the provision of Jesus to cleanse you from the sin, then it takes the wind out of the balloon of the enemy.

His demons are as helium balloons blown out of proportion to their power. They blow themselves up in an attempt to scare you into hiding, or running, instead of confessing and facing. The keys I have put into your hand to have victory over the demon is to face him with an attitude of humility, and knowledge of truth.

God Speaking in the Silence

A cork in a sink holds water in a place so things can be
washed. Sometimes, we need to put a cork in our preaching,
to allow the water to gather So God can do some cleaning.
Silence. The pressure that builds up behind the cork of a bottle
has a
purpose.
Don't be afraid
of the silence. When
we stop talking,
He starts.
There is reverence amidst the quiet. Everyone
knows. That's why they get uncomfortable.
They feel Him. God builds pressure when
we are corked. There is sure to be
something unstoppable when
it is released. Isaiah knew.
For, he had hid in a
cave.
There was an
earthquake,
a storm,
mighty
thundering.
Trees fell,
and rocks
slid
down
the
mountain.
Then, there was stillness.
It was then, that he wrapped his
cloak over his head and Came out
of the cave to talk to God. In the quietness,
he ironed out His issues with God. We do to.

93

Lego Your Ego

Lego your ego. Yugo mayhem with Him. Ego contorts meekness like a record in the hot sun. You don't sound right when you play your tune for others. And, you think it's the player.

So, you change churches. But, you are warped in your thinking. They see it. The ever so slight ripple in the black vinyl. They know why you don't sound right. And, you don't lego your ego. Freud built a whole kingdom on ego; self.

It is a slip, a slide, that leads to a spin out. Someone notices you don't sound right. They say that you don't sound happy. And, you start to question your own. You color your hair, work out, buy new lip stick. Then, you look in the mirror and ask someone else's opinion. He tells you that you need some changes. So, you trade in your glasses for contacts and loose 10 pounds. Then, you go back to him, seeking a favorable response.

Your circle becomes a spin. Pretty soon, there is no one that comes with you when you look in the mirror. You don't need him any more. You can find all your flaws without him. You are in the ego spin maneuver. You have gotten yourself into a place where you focus on yourself instead of what God wants for you. You need to break that record. For, it is warped and skips when played.

Come to Jesus and let Him cancel that record and give you a clean slate. Listen to His music that is already playing in your heart. He will give you your music. Listen. Then, you will become a record that plays without a player. Spontaneous praise to Him.

Twins of Humility and Reverence

Tantamount to your experience is your growth in humility and reverence. They are like twins. A boy and a girl. Who hold hands as they skip down the flower fields on their way to visit the neighbor's horse. For, you have found joy and communion amidst child like humility and reverence. You know that horse you visit is owned by your father, As it the field, the flowers and you.

is

94

Sing About Him

One thing that saddens our Savior: When we sing about Him instead of to Him. It is like inviting someone to coffee, then spending the time talking on the phone to someone else.

Quiet before God

Dream:

He wants to be in us like an Intra Aortic Balloon Pump. We wait on him with reverence. Speak quietly. He will come. They wondered what was the problem.

I said, "She is waiting for her IAPB. It will come."

Interpretation:

An IABP is a balloon that is inserted into the main vessel that comes off the heart. It is put there by a cardiologist when someone has heart problems and their heart is not pumping well enough to send the blood around the body strong enough to keep the person alive.

It has gas that is shuttled according to the heart rate. It keeps pace with the heart. Its job is to allow the heart to rest and heal. It decreases the workload of the heart by helping with circulation. It helps to energize the heart and heal the body.

When we wait on God with an attitude of reverence, it is like we become a mechanism of healing to the body. There is healing within the quietness as we wait on Him to speak to us before we pray.

Within the message of the dream, God says that He comes with the right messages when we are reverent and willing to be quiet before Him and listen. Some may be uncomfortable with the pauses, and they may wonder what is going on. But, God assures us, He is talking. Others will realize that He talks within the silence.

We Give Reverence

We give reverence, honor and respect to God for who He is. What He has done comes in a separate package called thanksgiving. And, the return demonstration is a show of passion. And, now in Church I don't worry about when others look at me. Because I know the display of unrestrained passion and love is something that doesn't come their way too often, A passionate love demonstration moves a whole group of people when it flows from a heart that is transparent. Openly in love with God. That is it. It doesn't matter if you notice the people are there. Praise is an interaction between you and God. There should be no difference between the way you praise God when You are alone with Him, and when you are in a group. Believe, me, they notice when you are standing right next to them praising God With an open heart. Passion for him spills over like a soda after it has been shook up. The heart is shook, stirred, and spills over with whatever He puts on it. For me, it's prayer. As, I praise God, my praise spills over into prayer for the body of Christ. I praise Him, I run into his arms, become swept up with emotion as He greets me once more with delight. How he loves to be praised! Then, He fills me up and over flowing. Then, the gift starts to get kicked into action. For me, it's prayer for the church. I sing until I can sing no longer. I go to the end of the road. I pedal the bike as far up the hill as I can, then I give myself over to Him and I pray in tongues. I am not very good in a choir because I become overwhelmed in the Spirit and the music continues after I have stopped singing. I can't. There is not enough air within my chest to do both. Once He sweeps me off my feet, I am swept. I pray what He tells me to pray. And the tears roll down my cheeks as I am touched to the core. My mascara runs, but I don't care. Then, I sing again. But, it's risky. Because, maybe tongues will continue. Prayer is praise is prayer. That is how it is with me. And, I can no more pray sitting, than I can sing sitting down. It doesn't happen. It is a matter of reverence. Because I know He is there. Just think? If we believe God, is there when we sing, what position would we assume? Songs are prayers. So, when I sing, I stand. It doesn't bother me anymore, that I am the only one. Because I know that what happens is when they see the love and passion of God flowing through my song, He speaks to their heart. When they see that I stand, not for them, but for Him, they, too stand. It is right.

For, they stand, not because they are told to by men, but because the are told to by the Holy Spirit. And, He has used my example of reverence to show them their need for more Reverence in their worship. For, it is impossible to hide passion for God. It is one of the things He uses to move His children closer to Himself. He loves to lead a group by moving the heart of someone passionate and in love with him. And, what happened? Those with similar passion ran to me after the service. For, they recognized a soul in love with their God who was brave enough to stand when He told her to.

Reverence at Worship

I am not glorified by your noise, But by reverence and truth. Church is not a pep rally, but a time of worship. For when you make noise, you cannot hear Me. When you cannot hear My voice, I cannot talk to you. Why should I show up in a meeting where the crowd Doesn't listen?

Meet Him with Reverence

Pitter, patter. A love beat plays song of my heart, love of my lifepitter, patter like feet walking down the hall, I sense Him coming. Coming to my door; to see if it is open that He may enter. The Holy Spirit is exciting. He is coming. Be quiet. Wait. Wait on Him and He will come. Wait with reverence.

Club for Cardiac Rehabilitation

Intensive listening is for active situations. It makes my heart burn. Burning hearts, over flaming love, overflowing passion. Overflowing into active love. What did you think? You could love a God this passionate and not feel His heart when it hurts? His passion is for those who hurt. Welcome to His club for cardiac rehabilitation.

A club For wounded hearts. Every heart comes with a spear in it, just like His. But, when given into the hand of His Father, overflows with blood and water, Forgiveness and healing through the Holy Spirit.

Filling Crevices of Pain with Snow

But, Father, I am a rocky top. Deep scars of life are etched into my face. My heart has been broken again and again as a small child. Drown in my tears on my pillow as I wept all alone into the Long dark nights. Sounds of pain echo in my mind. Torment of a lost child hood stolen by others. They had none of their own, so they stole from me. That is what wounded parents do. My summer came and went. Still, I was a rocky top, broken and forlorn, A pile of self pity, living in my own remorse.

At last a season for the fulfillment of His promises came. Winter. Snow fall from heaven. Blessed grace. It's not the first time it fell, but the first time I noticed it. My eyes were opened to see it in a new light. That Jesus they talked about was the same One who could help me. And, that winter in 1973, the snow fell, and I noticed it.

Jesus brought his forgiveness and healing into my life because I opened the door of my heart to Him. And those deep crevices of pain He as filled with His love. I'm pretty full, now.

Raising Our Flag

When we sing praise to the Lord, we need to attach our heart to His by the covenant of Jesus. It is our voice and His air. Because we don't own the air. We cannot provide air or make ourselves breath. But, we can hook our flag onto Him; onto His binding, His Covenant, then, we raise Him up. Our hands, our heart, our voice. It's not about octaves, but, reverence. Praise comes from the heart that lifts up the name of Jesus. What happens is that when we lift Him up, others pause as they see Him elevated in our lives. It's like raising a flag on a flag pole. When you raise it, they notice.

International Flags

There are International flags raised high On masts of mighty sailing vessels. Those set to sea, to bring provisions to places afar. To distant lands. The vessel is led by the flag, a passionate heart of reverence. He is a missionary.

Flag Heart Flutters

When we raise the flag, it becomes the entrance. Fill the flag with gentle gusts of wind. Extend the design into the breeze, and those nearby will gasp with delight. When we are filled with the Holy Spirit, the wind of God, and continue to extend ourselves in honor of Him, Like wind fluttering a flag. Heart flutters in the wind. Some hearts can Take more wind than others. These are ones that will fly higher. It's high flying passionate love of God atop a place for all to see. Elevated honor. A heart of reverence, flying with passion.

All Weather Flags

There are flags at night. Those high flying flags never loose their color, because there is a spot light to illumine the design. Day and night, the flag is raised and flutters in the breeze. Through storm, sun, and snow, it continues Undaunted by the weather. Why? These flags are made to fly More sturdier than others. They are individuals who have gone through tremendous experiences and witnessed the grace of God in unusual ways. He has pulled them through all types of weather in the past, So they know He will continue. High flying, passionate, tough, all weather flags. These type never come down. They are those who don't seem to need sleep, can go on for hours praising God, long after every one else has gone to bed. These are the tough ones. Why? Like Mary, they love more, because they have been forgiven more. *Bless them, Lord Jesus. Bless all the Marys, today. May I never mock a flag, no matter when it flies. Give me sensitivity for all types of ministry, all that lift their voice to praise Your name in reverence and honor.*

Singing Presents

When we sing before others, it is a presentation to God it becomes His present to them, when we allow His spirit to flow through us to them. It is the Same as praying for God to heal someone. We ask for the presence of God to change Their health. We present His presence. What a glorious present we carry! We are the presentation of His Presence to them. It is like He Has given us a cup to share. He gives us His presence Enveloped in the music. We sing and His presence fills us up, to overflowing, as it overflows, it spills onto them. *O glorious presence of God To flow through us! Flow from Your heart and back. An eternal circle.*

His Choir Lessons

The children have taught me how to release the restraint that was never supposed to be there in the first place. Unrestrained love. Sing heart, sing. Be released to sing for the Lord.

Sing from the Center

When someone uses all of his diaphragm to sing, the sound really comes out from the center of the heart.

True praise comes from the center. It cannot be pulled up by a choir conductor. It comes from a pure heart that is worshiping God from the core. We need to put the air behind the words. We push it from within, from the bottom of our being. The father provides the words for our praise, we provide the air. Praise is sent out with the power of the Holy Spirit, using our voice, his words, and our air.

Uninhibited praise is hard to find. It is characterized by sound being lifted into heaven through a prayerful heart, that sings from the center. Praise is prayer to God in the midst of the congregation. We simply pray to God, allowing others to listen in to our conversation. The more sure of the message, the individual is, the more powerful the prayer will be.

Praise from the center that meets our heart to the heart of God, moves those around us. Their spirit will be able to feel the spirit of the one who is moved as it draws closer to God.

Faith provides the bridge between quiet praise and loud praise. The person believes the message to be true and is not afraid to sing it out. Someone who sings loud praise knows that he has been forgiven and is not afraid to tell others. It becomes his testimony of his relationship with his father.

Father, give us a heart to praise you, uninhibited. Give us faith and a spirit of thankfulness for Your Salvation.

Salvation

When Jesus rose from the dead, He came to His disciples and showed Himself to them. Why? There is no mistaking that He rose from the dead, just as He said He would. What does that mean? He died. He permitted God to kill him The giver of life, allowed Himself to be overrun by evil to the point of death. How does that matter to us? He is a paver. He paves the road to God for us to also raise from the dead. But, because He paved the way, we don't have to go to hell, first. We can bypass that route and go from life to life. He knocked out a section of the track and replaced it with Himself. Like a train track that goes from one place to another, we can pass over Him. He has laid himself down, and allows us to pass over on the rails He has set. What are they, you say?

The rails of love and mercy with cross members of grace, Each step of the way we pass over another place where the Cross He died on brings victory. Place after place within our lives, He allows us to pass over because He pays the price for everything we mess up in. We are born with an intent to go against God. We immediately choose our own way and continue to follow that way until we die.It is our track and we cannot help it. We pass over sin by sin along our lives, building a track, laying a foundation for our own destruction. Our trellis is built on pride and rebellion.

We pick a direction based on our own needs and then pursue it. We do not have any innate regard for others. We become bent on the goals we set, and push off our track all that gets in our way. And, we hope. We don't know, though, because we cannot see into the night. We do not know what comes after death. So, we make up ideas. Reincarnation, levels of honor, outer space adventures. No one has come back from death to tell us…

No one but Jesus. Maybe we should ask Him. Oh, but if we do, there is responsibility. For, Jesus has called us not merely to know about Him, but to believe in Him. And what has He called us to believe? That He is who He says He is. God, the only one who can forgive sin. The only one who can pave the way, lay the track from hell and back to heaven By His blood. And, He has called us to do something with the belief that He died for us.

Not corporately, but individually. Personally. And, if we take it to heart that He died for us personally, then we must do something about it. We must ask Him to help us. help us to believe in Him. For, we cannot do it without His help. So, we call out for His help to believe in Him. But, He has not left us as abandoned children.

He has left us the Holy Spirit to guide us. And, just who is He, you ask? He is God, too. He is the Spirit of God that was given to us to assist us and keep us on the right track. And, how does that work, you say? Ask. For, when we ask for the Holy Spirit to help, He gives us understanding of who God is, who Jesus is and who He is. He gives us faith to believe in the salvation that Jesus has provided. Then, we can move along the track, not hindered by sin and death. But, you know we must die. Die to our own pride and rebellion. Die to doing things our own way. Die to trying to pay for our own sins. We claim unity with His ideas.

Then, we die to our old ways and experience new birth. Life through Him. The tree of life is planted within our souls. And, even though we may die physically, we will never die spiritually. Satan will not longer have control over us. We give control to God, get on His side, And the victory is ours as we join in the Kingdom of God. There is victory over death and sin.

We receive life, healing, deliverance, and unity with our Lord in a way that He has provided for. We pass over to the Lord, God, Almighty, on the rails of Jesus and are able to have free communication with Him. We become Holy as He is Holy.

We are freed from the bondage of sin. We have new life.

Jack in the Box Presence of God

What is it about a Jack in the Box that excites a child? The anticipation of excitement. The thrill of the unexpected. She knew it was coming. He would come out, but she didn't know just when.

She only knew that He would supply her with music until then. God sings His plans to us until He fulfills them. His time. We wait with eager expectation. It's always fun. Get ready to be filled with delight as He brings a new presence of Himself. He's coming out of the box that we stuffed Him into long ago. Surprise performance!

God Sings

God sings, too. And, it is He that opens our ears to hear his voice sing to us. His songs bring life to our spirit. It is foreign to us. Like a foreign language, we cannot understand it without his help. Lucky for us that He has provided special headphones to help us hear Him sing. Because it is a spiritual song, we need to have our spirit tuned to His channel to be able to catch the sound.

In order to be tuned to His channel and hear His singing, we have to have permission to enter His band. He has a special high frequency that only his children are allowed to listen into. So, we must first be counted as one of His children.

That's, easy. We simply believe that Jesus is God, died for our sins, rose again and lives at His right hand today. And, we ask Him to help us to join in this belief that Jesus died for us, as well. We become born again into His kingdom. Instantly, we become his children His kingdom is opened to us. He gives His children the keys to His kingdom. It's like your father giving you a key to the house. Because you have been born into the family, you are given privileges as a family member. One of the privileges of becoming a member of God's family, is to be able to hear His voice. Not merely, His spoken voice, but His singing.

He puts the key in our hearts to respond to Him. Yet, we cannot access this key unless we have the connector. It does not do any good to have a key, yet not know where the door is. The Holy Spirit can show us the way to the doors. He can help us to pass through the places where we need to go.

We enter the presence of the Lord on earth with a new song in our hearts. We can't learn it from someone else because it has never been sung before. It is new. When we respond to the promises of God given to us through Jesus Christ, then we are singing his Praise. It is music to his ears.

This is a special song put in our hearts to sing to Him when we were created. No one can sing it for us. It has never been heard before. It rings through the entire spirit world.

It cuts through everything created because it comes from the birth of our new spirit. The Angels lean forward to hear us and catch the key. These notes have never before been played. The morning stars sing together and the angels shout for joy with our spirit at the same time. We enter the Kingdom of God with singing to Him.

But, even while we do this, He is preparing to sing to us again. He is already preparing his response to us. We cannot out love Him.

The song of our heart is special because no other heart has known our pain and the rescue that has taken place. We have come through fire in our lives. There were times when we have given up. We know that we have done nothing to receive His grace. But, when we called out to Him, He helped us. He could have found a lot of other more important things to do. Mountains to move and Nations to run, but, He heard our cry and opened our eyes to see Him. He has given His love to us when we did not deserve it.

He has given us joy like water. It is an artesian well coming to us from the power of the Holy Spirit It bubbles up within us, and continues to bubble. As our hearts bubble for Him, they cannot be silent and must continue to sing because every song teaches us a new song. And, they all lead to His throne.

God takes delight in us and rejoices over us with singing. His heart is stirred when we have our sight given. When our paths are lit with his light. He loves to guide us with His song. It is His song responding to our song. Song to song in response to our service. He will quiet our singing to Him when He wants to sing to us. He quiets us with His love. He overwhelms us.

We are to invite others into our presence with God. Our presence of praising Him with songs. It is God's love song that brings unity to his Church. He calls us to speak the song He has placed in our hearts in the midst of others. The music flows from our heart. We are to come to God unashamed within the family of God.

The song that He has put in our hearts, is to the gift that He has called us to do. As we sing, the Lord will fulfill His purposes for us. It is the key He has put in our hands that opens the door for others to forward the Kingdom of God.

The demonstration of the gifts that He has put in our hearts will cause songs to break forth in others. Our motivation for the use of our gifts must be because we desire to sing for the One we love. We show our gifting to Him in the presence of others. Only then can He demonstrate His enduring love and faithfulness forever through all generations.

Our ministry must not be to others. It should be to him, because of what he has done for us, in the presence of them. They just watch us as we love Him. Only then will it be of eternal value.

When we step out with the song and sing it with all our heart, He will make His plans known to us and declare new things that have never before been shown. He announces them to those whom He can trust to give the message to others. When we listen to His voice, He will tell us His plans. He will tell us when He is coming to his people. Those who have learned how to walk in the gifting that God has called them to, will learn to recognize Him when He shows up.

They will be the first to see Him. Their job is to announce His arrival to others. Tell the children to pay attention, because God is here!

The procession into the sanctuary has come. In front are the singers.

Psalms 27:6, 30, 66, 100, 106.12, 138, Job 38.7, Isaiah 5:1, 35.6, Zephaniah 3, I Co 14, Ephesians 5, Col 3, Hebrews 2, Revelation 5.9, 14.3.

The Father Hums

My Spirit sings as I watch over you. My hand resting on your back as you snuggle in-between the soft sheets of your safe place. And I hum. Tunes meant for the one I love, my precious child. I sit on and on into the wee hours of the night. I suppose, I should go to My own place, but I like being here with you so much that I can't bear to go. So, I will stay just a little longer until day light comes and you are complete.

Free the Songs

Be My bird, be My hum. The song of your heart is the hum your spirit plays. Like a generator power locked meant to be freed through wisdom. There is a black out. Entire neighborhoods in darkness.

We think the generator is broken, but Satan has snipped the wires. Call the power company. There is a repair man standing by 24/7 to fix the areas of brokenness in your situation and repair the lines of communication. He is catty. A sly one. Deceptive guide who has a rulestick not of God.He has the wrong measurement in his hand. He is askew.

Hummingbird

Caterpillar spins the cocoon, not forever, but for a season. We toil and spin for our season, but soon we will burst forth with our new wings and fly. O winged one. Fly. Soar, O beautiful My heart flutters as you fly. When you fly where I send You, it's like a hummingbird goes from flower to flower. I gasp with delight, glee. You make your God to have glee, delight to let me provide you with my flowers. For a bigger yard. I pray, O Lord Mine have suckle for you to suck the nectar from. And I will lounge on the porch swing and watch.

And you were afraid I wouldn't notice. I planted the flowers and raised the hummingbird, Why wouldn't I notice when they matched? Drink the pollen and spread the rest. Be like a bee, be my honey. Be like a bird, sing. Sing of my Honey, my sweetness, my intimacy, the unity of your mouth with my sweet flowers. Suckle the nectar *to deliver it somewhere else. Be my Bee. Be mine*

Move the Hand that Loves You

Jesus Christ walked within a radius of only a few miles and changed the world forever. Changes are not done physically, as we move about in this world, but in the spiritual realm. For, when we pray, God's hand moves with lightening speed to act anywhere in the world. That is why a woman who prays in a rocking chair sitting next to some old faded lace curtains is the most powerful weapon against Satan that there is. For, when her heart touches God's heart, it moves His will, enacts armies, legions of Angels, and moves hearts of kings. So, when we are despaired, wounded, maimed, and unable to move, Pray. For it moves the hand of the heart that loves us.

Honor

The Dream:
I have a friend who thinks there are levels of honor. She knows, now, that I know, she has been taught wrong. It is not about levels of honor among men.

All honor belongs to God. He has called me to elevate His honor. I am angry because I withheld honor. Get to the bottom of this.

Interpretation:

There is a difference between honor from people and honor from God. His honor is righteousness demonstrated. When absolute righteousness is shown, then that is what is honored above all else because it becomes the standard that everything else is measured to.

The honor from people relies on their ideas of it. They pick a field, and when someone excels, they honor him. He is the best. God's honor system is based on purity. It is more like a virgin's honor. Purity in a relationship is one that has not been previously defiled by another.

With men, there can be many levels, because we don't see honor as absolute, but to be attained. With God, there is a standard, Jesus Christ, and His righteousness. We must attain to His standard to be honored by His Father. It is white and black. There is no grey area. Either we are pure and white, or we remain in our sins.

When we come to Jesus and ask him to wash us of our sins, we become white, not grey. Any time we ask, we become completely pure, like a virgin. We are made brand new. When we come to him, we honor Him by asking what He wants us to ask; forgiveness for our sins.

And, we are honored, as well, because He tucks us into His family and adorns us with righteousness. He puts it on us as a cloak, a garment, a coat. And we wear it. As long as we wear the coat of Jesus' righteousness, we will be pure, white and unblemished. We will be sinless before God, even while we are on the earth. In this, He is honored. Because we have assumed the position that we were meant to take. We have received grace and forgiveness through His blood sacrifice and are made pure as He is pure.

Jesus does not accept the praise from our flesh. We cannot offer adequate praise to Him when we do not have His love flowing through us. How can we know to praise Him, unless He teaches us?

God raises us up for the purpose of showing His mercy and displaying His power through our lives. It is by His compassionate mercy, that He raises one, and not the other.

We are His objects of mercy, which He has prepared in advance to demonstrate His glory to the nations. We are heirs of His promises through Abraham. It is not the natural children of Abraham, but is it the children of the promises who are regarded as offspring. We are His offspring because He chose to show compassion. The gentiles have obtained the position as children of God by virtue of receiving the gift of righteousness by faith in Jesus Christ.

Where God's glory dwells, He is honored. His honor comes with the glory.

We bring joy, honor and praise to God when we tell of the good things that He has done for us. For, when our lives are changed and we tell others about the true source of the victory, it brings honor to Him. Then, they learn about His love and mercy. Then, He can reach out to them and they will respond to Him as well.

When we are kind, we are honored. But, a prophet has no honor among his own family because they cannot see God's face when they are busy looking at the one they already knew.

As we learn to fear God, then we will gain a heart of understanding for who He is. As we learn who he is, we will start to see His mind in matters. We gain wisdom that is from Him. We combine humility with the wisdom that comes from God, to be honored by Him. Then, we truly are acting as He has. We are to let others praise us, not ourselves.

We wait on honor, because, then, we will know it is truly from God. The Father judges no one, but has entrusted all judgment to the Son, that all may honor the Son just as they honor the Father. When we don't honor the Son, we automatically do not honor His Father, who sent Him. It is like accepting me, but not my parents, who brought me up. The Father gave life to Jesus. He shared His life with us through Jesus. We need to remember that Jesus is the one who judges us because God has entrusted the judgment of the world to Him. And, just as God has given this privilege to Jesus, Jesus only judges with the information supplied to Him by the Father. They are related. We cannot accept one without the other. Jesus is God.

Jesus has honor because it has been given to him by God. He gave it to Him as He was willing to come to the earth, be crucified and sacrificed for our sins. Then, Jesus, gave honor back to the Father, as the ultimate provider of the plan for our salvation.

Our example of how to honor others is given to us by Jesus. We are to be devoted to one another in brotherly love and to honor one another above ourselves.

The honor that Jesus gives us is eternal life. He honors us by calling us His brethren. True righteousness comes from God alone, and flows from the Holy Spirit. He is the one who judges our heart. By our righteous heart, we are honored because we join in with Jesus. We become part of the family.

Psalms 8.5, 49.12-20,145.5, 149.9, Proverbs 3.16, 15.33, 22.4, 26, 29.23, Jeremiah 33.9, John 4, 5, 8, Romans 9, 12.10, II Corinthians 6.8, Revelation 19.7.

Heart Song Orchestra

To say I love you seems so trite when you are all I can think of day and night. My heart and spirit yearns to sing with you the tunes. The intertwining tunes. It's not a duet, but a symphony. It's like You hand me a microphone, then gather the team for one more song. The angelic hosts, the Father, the Son and the Holy Spirit. There's a complete orchestra when we sing. I don't even need to move my lips and the singing continues. Only to have my heart sing, then they all join in.

Why would I ever want to sleep? I don't.

Chapter V

Passion

A fire is started with a match. Match your heart to Mine.
 Find the place where your heart meets Mine.
That's a match made in Heaven by Me.

Passion

The Dream:

There is a group of 23 people in a room. Each person is given one index card (index cards like the ones I write verses and revelations on). We are to play a game. The game is who can steal the other person's card without them stopping you. I get 21 out of 23.

'Those with passion will win. They will get the most.' My daughter won the kid's version of the game.

Interpretation:

To me these cards are where I write what God is teaching me. It is His greeting card to me. His memo. His mailbag to me. His voice coming to me.

There are several types of 'cards':

Greeting cards can be given to another as a sign of love. These cards are used for interaction between us and God and us and others. The card displays God's program to us of events that are to happen in our life.

There is an identification card. It speaks of our role as a child of God. Identified with the family of God.

A card is a wire toothed instrument used to comb sheep. God sends his wires to us. The cards are Gods instruments (revelations) that are used to disentangle the fibers of the word of God. They untangle His plan for us from around the entangles of life. Then, He can weave His program for our lives. The comb grooms the sheep's fur.

We use what God teaches us through His words to groom the sheep, prepare the bride of Christ, the Church, for him (the groom). We comb through, look diligently, at what He desires to teach us to prepare us for compete righteousness to enter His Kingdom in Glory. This is part to the adornment of the Church in Christ's righteousness before His second coming.

In the dream, the game is who can steal one another's card without them stopping the other person. "Those with passion will win."

People don't care for God's word to them because they have not learned how to value it. Why don't they think it's precious like jewels?

The Holy Spirit needs to put the desire to know God in our heart. We ask Him how He desires us to know Him. He is displaying Himself everywhere. Often, we don't look. He has left billboards everywhere.

Why do I steal other people's cards? Because I see them as gems that I value. I care for the one who has left the gems. I would never leave something precious to my husband laying around. If I knew someone had his watch, for example, I would care for it because I know he values it. I value what he values because of my relationship with him. The same is with God's word. We value His word because He does.

This is God's word to them. He has busted through the heavens and mortality to talk to them. He has paid the price with his blood to get this message through to them. It is not just that He risked his life to get this message, He gave his life to get this message through. The cards are covered with the splattered blood of His Son, the one I love.

Not only this, God has promised that if we birth children after our own kind, they too will have the 'passion' and learn how to "win the Game'. We are called to reproduce: birth the next generation. It is the Holy Spirit that instills in them the desire to come to know the Risen Savior as their lover. We just provide the example.

Onions

Onions taste good and make your eyes water.
Just like the Holy Spirit. It's the presence of the cause.

Sing Soul

Sing, soul for His love is eternal.
Hallelujah! Let my praise ring!
Sing, heart, sing, overflow, Spill out.
Let that fill the air.
Nothing can tame a soul in love with Him.
The passion is from the Eternal one, the lover of my soul.
And, He just feeds it with His own passionate love.

Passionate Embrace of God

Is God always mellow? *Does the Spirit Always flow? The Spirit is a river. Sometimes it rushes toward His purposes just like a parent who picks up their child from a weekend at summer camp. There is a rushing into one another's arms, an urgent desire to return to the place of intimacy they had before he left for the week. The passion is released. Sometimes the urgency of God to be reunited with us releases His passion. It is just pent up energy. Those parents hold their child with the same tenderness and gentleness as they always have, only now there is an excitement, an urgency. In His zeal, God may draw us quickly, put us in the middle of a raging torrential river, but He always releases us into a pool.*

A story to compare: An analogy.

It is like the Father went to deliver the mail to us and the bridge was out over the river. He sent His Son ahead of Him to repair the bridge. There was a terrible battle with a Sea Monster. He won the battle, only to reach the other side and be killed by the natives who He was to bring the message to. They saw Him and were frightened because He didn't look familiar to them. He was a stranger. He died, but the bridge that He had spent 33 years building stood strong as ever.

It had mighty girders that went to the bedrock and strong timbers that would stand the test of time. This bridge would last forever. So the Father came across the bridge. He must step over the blood splatters of his Son. First, he picked up His Son and brought Him back home with Him.

But, then,   instead of
blowing that bridge   up, He used it to walk
back to those people that   killed His Son when He had
brought the first message from   His Father. Because of His
great love, He continues to come by His Holy Spirit, because
God is Spirit, across that bridge that is still splattered with His
Son's blood in an attempt to deliver   messages to us. Every
message is sealed with   a kiss
because He does not change. He   continues to love us.
Every message speaks of His   character because this is
the only means He has of speaking to us. It isn't a
perfect sound system   because our reception
isn't very good. Often we don't pay
attention; we   don't understand
it's Him   talking
to   us.

Sifting Sand

Ode to you A lost soul found by Me. I was walking on the beach.
I picked up a handful of the sands of time.
I sifted it through my fingers and I picked out a few grains.
To Me, one of the grains on the beach.
To you- your sand of time where you are your breath,
 your span because your span is but a breath.
O for you to make it My breath.
To be happy to beheld in My hand as I walk by the sea,
 humming the songs that well up within Me.

Persistence of God's Love

Passive persistence. Who said I am this? Satan. Deceiver of old.
That tricker, twister of My words. Passive; No. I am the only one
alive. He is dead, while I carry the breath to whom I will. Persistent:
yes. That part is true. For My love pushes me. Yes, even I am pushed.
It is the well within My soul that continues to break ground over and
over into hearts as they turn to Me. I persistently well up within My
children. But, there's no such thing as a stagnant well. For the well is
flowing water. Water from the snow melted for you from the reign of
My Son

Overpowering Love

*Elevation unaltered by human emotion. Joy, delight, glee,
jubilation, exhilaration. Enthralled by my love. You're like a 110 Volt
cord and I'm a 220 Volt. When I flow with My love through you,
yours becomes not noticed because mine overpowers it. How I love
you. Beyond all your ability to understand or feel. But I'll help you.
I'll be happy to over power you with waves of emotion, love, grace,
joy, mercy. Waves Just open the flood gates of your heart to Mine. Be
Mine.*

Holiness

Holiness is a place where God lives. Nobody gets to go there unless they are granted permission by Him. He can't be with us if we are not holy. Holiness comes through the righteousness of Jesus. When we claim His holiness, we wear His robe and can walk with God. Just like Adam and Eve in the garden.

When we are holy, then the Holy Spirit can come to live inside of us. We become the temple of God. Our heart becomes like the Holy of Holies in the Old Testament, where the glory of God lived among the Children of Israel. It is a place where we can meet with God on His level.

The Word of God washes us from sin. How does the word wash? It's like we stand under the faucet. When we get into the flow of His word it starts to wash over us.

It comes through us and we start to change. Our words mix with His out the other side. There is a mixing. The more we stay under the water, the more pure we become.

It's still some of us coming off. It's like hair dye that we wash off our hair after it is applied. We put our head under the faucet and try to get as much of the dye off as possible, yet we can't ever remove all of it before we dry the hair. There will always be some dye on the towel when we dry our hair. Each time we put our head under the flow a little more dye comes off.

The water becomes more and more clear as the hair continues to be washed. The cleansing of our soul with the Word of God is like that hair dye. The more we get into the flow of the Words, the more of our sinful nature gets cleansed. The Holy Spirit is like water. He cleanses us as we stay in the flow. The more we stay in the water (the word) the more clean we become. We become more and more pure with each cleansing.

Absolute holiness abides with God alone. He, alone, is Holy, and in the final hour, His righteous acts will be revealed.

We are in a process of holiness. We are holy and are becoming holy. As we grow, we are changed to become more like Him and less like the old sinful self that we were before. In the mean time, the deficit is filled with grace.

Holiness is possible through the Grace and Mercy package that was delivered by Jesus when He died for us. Grace enables us to be flesh, and yet be holy. Mercy stops the judgment of God from tearing us apart while we try to walk.

To be holy, all God asks of us, is to ask. We ask for the redemption through Jesus Christ. We come with a humble heart and ask for His cleansing of our soul. He promises to make us Holy. We can stand before Him, here on the earth because He has made the provision for us to be perfectly holy now.

Proverbs, Job, Ecclesiastes, Romans, Hebrews

Heart Winner

With everlasting loving kindness I have chosen you above others to be My child. You don't need to do anything to live up to it. You are. Just as I Am. You exist because I exist. I created you. Not once, but twice. For, when you Came to me and ask, I gave you new birth. Then, I welcomed you into the new world, My Kingdom. And, then you looked up. You raised your eyes and looked up into the horizon. You didn't look as others do. You didn't focus on my Son, the way He used to be. You looked for Him to rise, like the sun. And you camped out, waiting, watching, persistent, determined. And, I gave you things that were not yours. I have piled onto your plate food that others rejected. My Words that were given to others, they threw out, into the trash, because they didn't care for My heart. You, my love started there. By learning to care for My heart, You win. The prize. My heart. Wear it proudly, like a necklace. Adorn your life with My heart. And, all will see it and know it's true. You need not make any excuses or acknowledge that they wonder. Because they don't. I have put it into man to know that I am. Remember, I created them, too.

Spin Out

The dream:

I am in a car. My father has called me up and asked me to help him move from one house to the next. We load some stuff into the car and start out. It is night and the roads are windy. We are following a fire truck. We are in a small family sedan. My father is in the front seat along with my brother and I am in the back seat behind my father

My father is in the driver's seat, but I am driving the car. We all have steering wheels. I don't have any pedals for gas and brake, but I have an emergency brake. The road is windy and it is dark out. I can barely see over my father in the front seat. I loose sight of the fire truck.

All of a sudden there are some black trash bags in the roadway. I try to stop the car but loose control. I can't find the brakes. I hit the trash in the road and we go into a complete spin ending up with one wheel hanging over a steep embankment.

As the car is careening out of control, I yell at my father in the front seat, urgently to steer the car from the front seat. Up until now, I didn't notice that He had a steering wheel. He and my brother have made no effort to drive up to this point. He has been sitting back with his arm over the seat.

He comes to alertness and is ready to take the steering wheel, but I never give him an opportunity to drive the vehicle, because I am overwhelmed with fear. I use my emergency brake to stop the car. Panic has overwhelmed me as I spin out of control attempting to drive the car from the back seat.

Interpretation:

It's my Father's move, yet I contend with Him to drive. In this dream I am found guilty of trying to steer my Father's vehicle from the backseat. I am a backseat driver and I spin out. I drive the car by manipulation from the back seat. I have told God that I want Him to run my life, but I haven't given Him the opportunity to take the wheel.

I continue to steer by manipulation from the back seat.

When I pray, I am contending with God, thinking that I already know the outcome. I just look around Him and follow the what leads to the fire, the truck.

But, the message of the dream is that the Holy Spirit will not take control if we don't permit Him to. The fire engine relates to someone going to a fire. I am seeking the 'fire of God' and going in the right general direction. But, when I do not rely upon the Holy Spirit for everything, my own trash gets in the way. I cannot see into the darkness with my physical eyes, therefore I need spiritual eyes to direct me.

My pride told me that I could see 'over' my Father into the path that the car was going to go. I am overlooking His direction for my life. Darkness overwhelmed me and I spun out. When, I am overwhelmed with crashing from going the wrong direction, I call out to Him, yet I keep control. I use the only control that I have left, which is to pull the emergency brake. It is the only thing I am given in the back seat of this vehicle.

The only control that was left was the emergency brake, which is my will to 'stop'. God does not take our free will from us. He does not grab control in our life when we loose control because our own will, pride, trash, and spiritual blindness that causes us to spin out of control.

He will not tolerate us doing ministry in His Kingdom by manipulation from the back seat, either. He desires for us to turn over freely the control of the ministry in our lives to Him. He needs to drive us. Our only recourse is to be driven by Him, or put on the emergency brake (bail out of it altogether).

I am not in the right position to see the road clearly, and to steer clear to the trash ahead. I have put myself above my brothers and my Father (Pride and Idolatry of self) thinking that I could control the whole car from the back seat. When I try to drive from the back seat, I cannot do it. I am bound to crash, taking my brother with me.

In the dream, the father doesn't have a brake in the front seat, I only have an emergency brake. In true, God doesn't have a brake, because He always longs to pursue a relationship with us, it is we who brake from Him, often when our life gets out of control and we don't turn the wheel over to Him. I cannot take His plan and my own heart. I have to allow Him to control my heart. Only God's love can drive me, nothing else, or I am found to be in the driver's seat by manipulation.

If I have been given the heart of God, How do I let God's heart drive me? Let go of the wheel, ask for help, trust in His Word, listen to His Voice, obey.

Notice that the father never jumped out of the car, even when it was spinning out of control. He just waited on me. He never leaves us. What I need to do is give up 'my vision' for God's Vision. Only He can see the road. A spirit of hypocrisy, self indulgence and uncleanness compels me to think that I am worthy to drive the car above my Father or my brother, even though they are both in the front seat and have steering wheels.

Job 32.8, 32.19, 36.16, Psalm 119, Isaiah 51, II Corinthians 5:14.

Passion and Lust

Passion and Lust. What's the difference? There is intense feelings and an emotional release of pent up energy. Passion is the base. The intended purposeful direction of the emotional outburst. To love God. Lust is the counterfeit bill. It warms your own pocket, but won't buy anything on the real market. It has no resale value.

Free Bird

A passionate singing heart soars.
Lets go, Quits flapping his wings, and soars in the updraft of God's fire. It's dancing above the flame in the wind.
The breath of the Holy Spirit.

The Heart Trainer

Dream:

I'm in a bus with my supervisor, and others. We are in recliners. She can't sleep. She asks me if I can sleep. I say that I love to sleep. I go over to the side and find a recliner to sleep in. A train goes by.

Interpretation:

The Lord tends His flock like a shepherd tends His sheep and holds us close to His heart. His instruction is like words whispered into our ear by some one who loves us tenderly. He holds the keys to help us understand what is going on.

He has not abandoned us and He has never ceased to provide guidance to us. He has given us the Holy Spirit as our trainer. Just like when God led the Children of Israel out of Egypt, He has provided us with a pillar of Cloud by day and a pillar of fire by night. He will make Himself visible to us, but we have to look His direction, His way.

To get instruction from God, we must learn how to listen with our heart. Our heart has 'eyes'. It can see. The other day, I asked someone how they were.

Their reply was, "OK."

My response was, "Your mouth is saying OK, but your heart is saying, 'I am not well.'"

All of us have experienced being around someone who is sad. Maybe they recently lost a loved one. This makes for a sad heart. It can be felt. It is different from 'seeing' with our eyes. It is a feeling that is picked up by our heart.

When a heart is happy, all will feel it. When a heart is heavy, everybody knows. This is an avenue that we do not use unless we nurture it by God's help. It is a 'God Level' of seeing. We can pray for the 'eyes' of our heart to become open to God. If our eyes are open, it makes us sensitive to the things of the spirit world.

It makes us aware of how God's Spirit is responding to our spirit. Next, if we want to seek His wisdom, we need to pay attention; fix our gaze on the heart of God. This is about not being afraid to pursue the heart of God with our heart. Eli was replaced with Samuel as a prophet because God wanted someone who would, not only tell them His words, but care about what was on His heart. He wants us to care about the things that matter to Him. His heart issues.

Chase the Truck

Then, we can grow into understanding. Understanding takes more work. We have to chase it like chasing down a speeding Semi truck. We need to pick up speed (do what we know we are already supposed to do) then pace ourselves. We need to pace ourselves with the truck in front of us, which is the understanding. Do what we understand that God wants us to do. Do it.

Then, we need to become persistent in catching that truck. If God gives us a dream, then be persistent to press God until He gives understanding. If God gives a message, then press Him until it is clear what He wants done with it.

God values persistence when seeking Him. He will reward those who diligently seek Him. In order to catch that semi, we have to lighten ourselves to run faster. We must let go of everything that weighs us down from seeking God with all our heart, soul and strength. Then stretch forward.

We must reach out into the mind of God in places where we have never gone. Believe a vision, believe a dream, believe the 'small voice' in our head. Then, watch as the truck gets closer, for just like God, it will suck you forward towards it. As we move toward the will of God, He will suck us forward into Himself. We will be absorbed before we know it. He will become our life. His breath, His word, His wind will pull us in; His love draws us.

But, that is not the end of the journey. For, only when we pass the semi-truck and get in front of the truck will we be able to look into the future.

The truck symbolizes 'now' in our life. We want more than 'now'. It is good to have God's direction for now, but it is awesome to have His direction for 'next week'. When pass Him; allow His shadow of glory to pass over us, then His presence will combine with His word. There will be a collision of the Scriptures, the words of God for today and His presence. The three fold combination will provide us direction for the future. The glory pass. It is the shadow of the wings of God.

The Train

Our heart is to be applied to instruction and our ears to the words of knowledge. We are to listen to God with the eyes of our heart and to His words with our spiritual ears. When we see something with the eyes of our heart, we can apply our heart to it.

Our vision with the eyes of our heart should direct the heart. Then, the heart should direct our mind, which leads our flesh by discipline. God has given us His Spirit so that we may understand what He has given us. He expresses spiritual truths in spiritual words. He has given us an interpreter; the Holy Spirit to help us understand. The truths come from God via the Holy Spirit to our spirit into our heart.

The connections between all the elements need to be unclogged. Then, they can be understood by our mind, because he has also given us the mind of Christ. That mind of Christ becomes activated through knowledge, wisdom and discipline pressing into what He has for us.

God knows that the true desire of our heart is to find unfailing love. This is what He wants to provide to us. When we listen to Him, He will teach us how to become true to our heart. We need to ask Him how to experience it here on earth. We won't experience it using the same techniques that we use with other relationships. We can recognize the instruction of God; it always leads the heart first.

God wants to go where we hide; where we draw back to. He wants to become our secret place.

When we run to Him as our secret place, He will deliver us from all of the evil thoughts that torment us. He will, not only deliver us from the enemies, but He will direct us in which way to go to conquer them. Then, He will watch over us, ready to intervene as we call out to Him.

He doesn't just send out His instruction, then go back to heaven. He stays with us every step of the way as He has given us the Holy Spirit as our continual guide.

We need to listen to God to tell us when to plow, when to plant and when to harvest in the Kingdom of God. He knows the seasons and will instruct us in the right way to plant, nurture, and harvest the crop. He wants His kingdom built and His children to be nurtured. We can learn about God, but He wants us to know Him for ourselves.

There is a proper time to do everything and only He knows when. We need to listen to Him for the prompts. His instruction comes through His counsel. It is an interaction between the Scripture and the word of God. When God gives us instruction, all of His power is behind His word.

The Scripture is given to us to help teach us the ways of God. It is like a sword at our side. The Holy Spirit will help us to become trained to use that sword at the right times. The true treasures within the knowledge of God are in the understanding of the Kingdom of God.

God speaks to us; He instructs us with visions and dreams in ways that we often do not understand. He continues to speak to us, even though we are like small children who have not yet learned His language. He wants to teach us His language. He will continue to give us lessons. We need to take notes. God will provide counsel into the inheritance that he has given his children. He places the counsel into our heart.

Often He will instruct our heart in the night time. When our heart is in tune with His heart, He will bring instruction through His heart into ours.

Without God's instruction to us, we are like doves in the midst of a howling desert without water.

He has come to provide us with His words to direct us. They will guide us, shield us, care for us, and guard us as the apple of His eye. His words are like an eagle that stirs up its nest and hovers over its young, that spreads its wings to catch them and carries them on its pinions. He will nourish us as with honey.

The source will seem very unlikely and no one will believe that God is 'talking to you'. Like honey from a rock it will seem.

Deuteronomy 32.10, Job 33, Ps 16, 32, Proverbs, Isaiah 8.11, 28,40, Nehemiah 9,Mt 13.52, I Corinthians 2, II Timothy 3.16.

Unrestrained Tenderness

Socially eloquent, intuitively astute, beautiful is your face with tears on it as you praise Me. A heart touched because you love Me. I see those tears. I count the sodium in the salt that flows down your face. Believe Me, I notice. Believe, you Me, so do they. A hungry heart in love with her Lord doesn't come their way too often. It's moving. Unrestrained tenderness is from Me. It's Mine. You learned it from Me. A good student learns from her instructor. His tenderness abounds within His bounds

Blessing at the Table

Dream:

Wait until everyone is at the table, then we focus on the gifts He has brought us. We thank Him for them. Then, we say the blessing.

Interpretation:

A gift is something that is given to someone to show their love. It must be opened to see what is inside. The gifts from the Holy Spirit are to be opened in his presence to show appreciation for what he has given; just like Christmas. When we receive gifts from others, the family all sits in the living room and opens their gifts.

Part of the excitement of the season is to watch the person's face as they open the gift that has been given. We look for the delight displayed in their face when they see what the gift is. If there is a family party, it is rude to take the gift into the bathroom and unwrap it on our own. We would never think to do this.

Notice, also, that there is just as much delight on the face of the giver as the one who gets the present. A child, for example, who has made an art project at school, can't wait to have their mother open the present. They are pent with excitement, and will, often, attempt to rush Christmas, to get the parent to open what they have made.

Why? Because when children make gifts, they put a piece of themselves into it. They are thinking about their mother the whole time that they color that picture. They give from their heart. So, they can hardly wait to share the demonstration of the gift which tells their mother how much they love them.

Then, of course, we tack it on the refrigerator with little magnets for all to see. It is a proud display of an intimate relationship between our children and us. No one could disprove it, when it is on display in the kitchen.

Our Heavenly Father has given us gifts. He has colored us pictures of His love. They are demonstrations of His love to us; they are a piece of Himself on paper. He wants us to open these in His presence and in the commonality of the rest of the family (of God).

He is waiting for us. We must come through the door into the house. We enter into his presence through the blood of Jesus. We have to become open to what He wants for us to receive; open the door, and take a risk to enter into whatever is waiting for us on the other side of it. Calling on the Name of Jesus is the key to this door. God has put a little 'call box' just outside the door on the porch. If we stand on the porch and call to Him, He will answer us. He stands just inside the door and beacons us to enter, just like we are already family. He has left the door open to us through inserting the key. We need only to push.

In the dream, there are white china plates with a silver trim. They have been washed to glisten. There is gold silverware and a white table cloth. A bouquet of purple lilacs sits in the center of the table.

It is like a dinner party. Each of the places have a name tag, so that we know where we are to sit. It's a round table; We are all equally special in his eyes. He treats us as if we are his 'only' child. After all, that is who we traded places with. His only child was taken, so that we might become His children.

The Lord wants to bring us to His banqueting table. He has all kinds of wonderful things for us to eat. He has been in the kitchen preparing blessings for us; things to give us. He gives us His presence, His food, which is His word, and His gifts.

Often, we come to His presence, the table, and we dine on His word, but we do not open the gift that is left by our plate. What are the gifts? The gifts are what ever God gives us. He has set before us things that are to be shared with others. There have been times when I given a box of candy to someone. I give them a box of candy during the party, because they have previously told me not to give them anything.

Like my grandpa, they say, "Don't give me anything. I don't need anything. Just come."

Yet, I still feel compelled to show up with a gift. I cannot come without one, so, I bring candy. The reason that I give them a box of candy, is because I know that they will enjoy sharing it with everyone who is there. And, if it all works out as I planned, they will not have anything to take home with them. I have tricked them; I have given them a present and they bring nothing home. It is a present to give to others.

Other times, I have brought two boxes. The one, I give openly, to the person. He shares it with the group. Then, later, in private, I give the second box. The group has had their fill, and the individual has felt that he has shared. He is not obligated to share any more. This one he can take with him for himself.

The gifts that God gives us are like the second illustration. He gives us and keeps on giving. We can freely share the 'candy' that He gives us because He has back up stock and will keep giving us boxes.

The dream says that 'we are to wait until everyone is at the table, then we focus on the gifts He has brought us.' The gifts that God has given us are His presentation. We are to present Him to them. We demonstrate His faces. They can come to know Him better when we show them who He has shown us, He is. We are His artwork. He wants us to pin it to the refrigerator. Sometimes, I receive gifts that are personal. They are the most special ones by the ones dearest to my heart. When I am given lovely floral underwear and I open it in front of others at the party, I get embarrassed. The reason I get embarrassed is because it shows everyone there how intimate the person is with me that gave me the gift. If someone knows what color of underwear I like; that is intimate.

Similarly, we receive gifts from God that are personal. We hesitate to open them in the presence of others because, then, they will know how intimate we are with Him. We are 'embarrassed' about the intimacy of the relationship. No matter how we try to hide it, we can always tell who loves who at party where gifts are given. It is evident on the faces of the one receiving the gift and the one who gave it.

The same is true with God. When we share with others what He has given us, it is immediately evident to all the level of our intimacy with Him. They can see how well we know 'each other'.

It is His goal for all to know Him better. Part of the way He is known is by the show of His gifts. So, share what He has given.

This gives thanks to Him for the gift, and blesses the rest.

High Breed Passion

High breed passion exits from a thorough breed horse with a passion to race for the crown. Unbridled passionate love.

Father, give us a passion like a thorough breed, that we may run the race with the speed You put into our hearts. Give us passion to love You; unbridled passion. Passion to love others the way You do. Amen.

Reach Out to Others for Help

Is your goal just out of reach? Stretch. Not that way, the other way. Look for the bridge. When God gives us a goal, and it looks like He has not provided the provision to meet the place where we long to be, we need to open our eyes. He never intended His children to be like race horses with blinders on. We are not meant to run our race alone. Even Jesus did it. Mary birthed Him, Joseph hid Him, Magi introduced Him, Mary anointed His body for burial, and another helped him to painfully lug that cross to His death. If Jesus needed help to attain the goals His Father laid out for Him, Why wouldn't it be that we also should work in cooperation with others to get where we are supposed to be? I guess the question remains. Who will help me, Lord?

Fun Passion

Passion that is the most fun is taking the elevator from the basement to the sky tower in 0-40. Moving quickly into the presence of God. Running quickly into the arms of your Father. You have to be ready. If you are not, you may start out with the intent to take the elevator to the top and find yourself stalled out at ground level. An open heart opens the shaft that provides the way. Jesus' blood offers us the opportunity to come freely into His presence.

So, Go into the ground level, your knees, your face, park yourself, and put on your coat of righteousness, enter the combination that opens the heart of God. And, hold on for the ride. Soar to the top of the passion of God's love.

Race Horses

The race is run with Jesus as our friend. Like a couple of race horses; brothers at birth, we run. Because, He is our brother, we want Him to win. So, we drop back a half step to give Him the lead. But, He wants to give the victory to us, so He drops back a tad. My forward motion pushes Him and He pushes me. Each desiring the other to be victor, win the crown and be declared the winner. And, we will.

For, He has declared it a tie from the beginning of time. As we are bound to Him with an eternal covenant, the tie stands. We both win. The crown is ours. Victory waits. Yet, we run. For, the race, the companionship, the acceleration of the plan. Burst of excitement, exhilaration of the exercise at such speed. And, we know, at the finish line, we will both flop down in the grass and roll with laughter and joy. Exhaustion, mixed with an eternal high.

High Breed

You can be a High Breed, a beautiful white glistening thorough breed that was specially bred for this run, this race, this event. Run, My child. Go. Don't worry that others won't be able to keep pace. Let Me be your pacemaker to move your heart toward Mine. Like a hybrid white tea rose, your fragrance is pure, your stance is elegant, your dance wonderful. For you prance and dance all the way to the finish line. And, you know there's a cup waiting for you. Drink the cups of grace along the way. The cups of mercy and love. Feast on tender grains of My word and delight in the Holy Spirit. Run, race, sprint, gallop, because, Love, I will be there to pass out the ribbons and party with you at the finish.

Pressing Tenderness

Jesus is the one that erases the errors in our life. Through the pages of our time, we leave our mark. Many times, we press too hard, tearing holes with Our math. Many times, we have fallen asleep, leaving a trial of sagging letters. At times, our pen nearly ran out. Our lantern almost snuffed out because we were not paying attention. For, we haven't valued the paper, the stationary that God writes on. Our heart is the pad He uses to convey His messages to us. But, we have not cared for it. We have not allowed Him to press with His Tenderness on the hard places of our heart.

Heart Song

You are the beauty of my adornment. I provide the Clothes, you provide the color, the hue, the tone. Your life through My grace plays the tune. It is a tune that others would give all they have just to see once in their lifetime. Do not underestimate the value of your heart as you play My heart tones. I harp. I am the harp you play. Play it like an angel. Be faithful to be sent to serve others. As a harpist cannot focus on the audience, you must focus on the song, not the instrument, although, it is beautiful. It is still just an instrument. The gift of wisdom is your instrument. But focus on the song I play in your head as your heart is in tune with mine. Heart song. Don't talk, sing. Mellow melodies of My love and give them like toasted marshmallows on the reed. The reeds are in the marsh, the place where the Spirit flows up from the ground by the well that has been provided. But, as you hold the reed in your hand, skewer the marshmallows and toast them. Pick up My word, write it down, then carry it into My presence. Allow Me to put My passion on just the right places and hold it there. Be still, calm, mellow, like a harpist.

The Margin of His Grace

Above the margin of your error My grace flies. Outside the parameter of your ability is where I live. You must cross the line from possible into impossible to be on My side. Of course, you can always choose to stay on your side, within the boundaries of what you can do without My help. But, then, you don't need Me, do you? And, whose stuff are you doing? Mine or yours? The place where My grace meets you is like a cliff. Your toes hang over. Like a high dive, you are out there and there is no backing down. You teeter for a while, in full anticipation of a belly flop into the pool. As long as you are willing to stand there, extended for what you know to be true, I will sustain you. Will you fall? Will you jump? You don't know how to jump and I will not permit you to fall. You are a sturdy as if you were on the side of the pool. That is it. You picture where you are using My perspective, not yours. Because I picture you walking where I told you to go. I created mass, air, gravity, and water, you are safe, no matter where you are.

130

Take the Plunge
into the Pool of God's Love

The books are not fruit for others. They are to show them how to find the ice box to get their own fruit. What I have is like a high dive. You follow the steps and climb the ladder.

You can choose the low dive, or head for the high dive. I have taken the high dive.

I have chosen to press God for all I can get. I believe His word as He speaks into my spirit day and night. I climbed and launched off the spring board into the pool of His understanding, revelation, wisdom and counsel. But, it's a high dive.

It puts me way out on a limb. The limbs are where the fruit is. But, the limbs are also the place in a tree where you can see through the branches the most.

It is the place where the tree looks the most fragile. But, it's not. The most Flexible places in a tree are on the Boughs. The Books are like swim instructors To coax Others onto their own swim platform.

Airmail Love

Elevated above the angels is your love to Me. For, your love is sent to My throne like a hot air balloon with its many colors. The passion of your heart lights the fire that ignites the flame to fill the balloon with billows of air. Not oxygen, for oxygen does not enter my Kingdom. It's a spiritual place. Filled with your prayers, the balloon floats straight down the hall of My palace, and into My throne room. Your love for Me, provided the envelope. Just like mail delivered to a king. Airmail.

Sweetness in the Garden

The Dream:

I plant a garden. Things come up that I didn't plan on. I didn't know that I planted that. There's yams (sweet potatoes). They are huge and white. They already are covered with marshmallow sauce and brown sugar while they are growing in the ground. They were ready to put into the oven. Ready to serve. There were other fields that were empty. They have yet to be planted. I wonder why I left them not planted. I realize that there are vegetables that I didn't know I planted. I must have planted them or they would not have grown from those seeds. I guess I didn't know what kind of seeds I had.

Interpretation:

As I go along, I plant with the seeds that God has given me. I don't have any way of knowing how far He chooses to expand His Kingdom and His Word. As I am going along, I am planting stuff I never dreamed of. The sweetness of God, grown from His seed, produces supernatural size vegetables. They grow up with His sweetness in them right from the start. They are complex carbohydrates. They are far more complex than I give them credit for. His word seems simple to me, but it is very complex and topped with His sweetness, ready to serve others. It is His sweetness ready to be picked and served.

My Heart Song

Above and beyond, in and through
You are my heart song, and I love you.

Expired, Outdated, Dreams

We are a distribution company. Large scale, long haul, heavy movers, overnight delivery service. But they won't open the boxes. Why? The stamps are wrong. They think it's outdated. They need To turn the box over because there's lots of stamps. God is giving us dreams. We think that if we have had them a long time ago, they are outdated. He has made them to be good for any time that they are opened. He has placed many stamps on them for different times in our lives. *Because my boxes have been returned and sent several times over. And I paid the price for service. Postmark paid in advance. Jesus. The ultimate Christmas box.*

Elevator of God's Presence

Anticipation is my enemy as I feed on the goodness of God. I take the elevator to the penthouse of the tower His love. What a view! A gasp of rapture delight to be so close to the one I love. So, as I move into His presence each time, I look for the elevator to reach that level as before. But, I never anticipated that I was in a different Building Starting from a different place within the story. Because my walk is a process. The buildings are along a hill, a mountain. And, I believe I started in the valley of despair. So, when I went to the third floor, at that time, I was sure I was in heaven. But, today, I think I am in a different building, being moved further up the Mountain toward His Holiness. So, when I ride the elevator to the third floor, I think Hey, this is only the Third floor. But, actually, it a mile higher than before. That is how God is. He kind of tricks us into increasing closeness, so we don't get scared and run off. Remember. That is the Fear of the Lord.

Joy and Presence

Dream:

There are two kinds of dish washing liquid. The brand is called Joy. They are very large containers. One is yellow and the other is orange. I am trying to tell the difference between then. I decide to taste them. I taste the 'Joy". Then, I read the label. I think that when I taste it that it will foam in my mouth, but it doesn't. I am wondering which is the real Joy.

Interpretation:

God washes us. We are like containers that can be filled with good things from God. We need to be clean, just like dishes, before we can expect to be used as containers to serve others. We need to be clean plates to be able to serve others. God writes His word on us and He uses us to serve others. We turn ourselves over to the hand of the dishwasher and be cleaned at the sink. He wants to wash us, cleanse us, and make us sparkle. It is by His hand that we are washed under the running water.

The message in the dream, is to use soap. Soap connects a positive ion with a negative ion. It is the link between positive and negative. When we are cleansed, God not only uses water, He uses soap. He takes us and washes the negative aspects from us, then, replaces them with positive ones. He is the link to make our sorrow into happiness. He takes the very things that have caused us grief and turns them into ministry. When He does this, a joy rises up within us. There is a cleansing.

But, there are two cleansing that come our way if we watch and wait. The first cleansing is when we are forgiven for our sins. We come to the foot of the Cross and ask Him to cleanse us. When He does, we overflow with joy. We were slaves to sin, but now we are free. The freedom of our once bound soul, causes gladness to overwhelm us.

A second joy is available for those willing to go a step further and God to for total healing. He wants to heal us, but we stop short of it. For healing, the wound needs to be reopened and the infection needs to be taken out of it. All of the infective processes of the enemy that were put there into the wound, need to be replaced by the grace of

134

Jesus. We need to deal with our past.

Weights that encumber, keep us from accepting the second joy. The race is easier to run without weights. We need to give them to Jesus. He paid the price. When we release this weight, our heart will be released to sing. Our heart can't sing with Jesus' heart if it wearing handcuffs. It needs to be released first. Only when we get a hold of both of the joys, can our heart be released to praise.

Our praise is being held by things unknown to our present mind. By the stripes of Jesus we are healed. He was beat so that we won't be. It's the 40 stripes. They encircled His whole body. He doesn't take our weights, we let them go. His arms are already extended to take them.

Often, our wounds have healed over with scar tissue. They are crusted over; filled with granulation tissue. We see through scales. Our scales need to fall from our eyes. Our own weights on our own scales. We need to stop weighing our own lives with our own scales. Hold them up to His scales. Let Him weigh them.

When we release these pains to Him and allow Him to open the door on them to heal them, it is like a huge steel door of a penitentiary will be opened. We have been imprisoned by our own values. We need to let go of them. Let Him give our past experiences His value. When we turn them over to Him, He will re value them with His weights and give them new meaning in the Kingdom of God.

They are the things that become 'testimony' to others of God's greatness. Only then do we become aligned with His mold for our lives. He will provide the key to the lock. Then, the door will open with a rumble and a crash. He will turn ashes into Joy. This is the second joy which frees the songs.

Joy links the anointing to the presence.

We have been chosen by God for a purpose. When we start to walk toward that purpose, then we are walking into the anointing He has predestined us for. The presence of God is when He shows up. There is immeasurable joy when we start to walk into what God wants us to be and He is there with us. A threefold cord is not easily broken.

When we put ourselves where we are supposed to be, His presence will come to us.

When we tell our Child to meet us at a specific place in the Mall, then we will be there at that time to meet Him. God is like that. When we listen to His voice and walk in the direction He tells us to, He will be there waiting for us. He is our Father who will be waiting at that designated spot where He has instructed us to go. *May we be faithful to listen to Him and be there on time.*

We cannot manufacture the presence of God and sell it to others.

As much as we desire others to be in the presence of God, it is an individual thing. The only way that the presence of God shows up is when we press into Him. We have to open ourselves up to Him, then, He opens himself up to us. He meets us at that point. His presence will meet at whatever level we are willing to go. When God shows up, He brings all of Himself. He is the great revealer of all of the things that are secret. If we have things that we want to keep secret from Him, then we will back off when He gets too close to those special areas that we are trying to hide.

Of course, we can't really hide things from God, only from ourselves and others. But, we play mind games. Fear keeps us away from being brutally honest with ourselves and Him. If we tell Him all those 'secrets' then we have to deal with them. We find it painful to go over our 'sin pile'.

So, we stall and pick through taking the least painful first, then working downward until we can bear it no longer. After all, it is embarrassing to get naked before Him.

So, that is the problem. Even though we may be eager for the presence of God to come to us, the person next to us may not be so eager. We have no way of knowing the things that will be revealed to them when God shows up. That is up to Him. Perhaps, there are things that He has told them to do and he has rebelled and gone his own way. He needs to deal with that first.

God initiates the interaction between us and Him. He is always eager to come to us. We hold Him back. There is no substitute for Him. We cannot manufacture anything close. If we try, it will just be painfully short of who He really is. Emotion is not the Holy Spirit moving among his people. Others will not buy this as from God. Their spirit bears witness that it is not the Holy Spirit. They all know a fake.

If we get caught selling the presence of God to others, He will judge us for it. We must turn off our own flame and burn His. Pass by the stage

God is not a stage show. He does not dwell in 'hype'. We need to come into His presence with reverence recognizing that we are all saved by the same grace. We need to pass by the stage show. God does not show His presence when we know it. Only, when we are so absorbed in Him, in the awe of Him, will He be shown through us. We won't even know it.

His Passion Lives

What does life and liberty have in common?
Nothing.
They are only promises through Jesus Christ meant to be fulfilled through His blood.
Nothing common about the blood of Jesus shed for us. One great feat will cause one great defeat for all our enemies.
His death to give life. His passion lives to give liberty.
Theoretically speaking, it is not possible how one man's death could bring about the victory of all God's children over sin.
God is not merely a great thinker.
He is also a doer.
He thought the plan through to victory before He did it.

Prison Break

You are a heart that was never meant to be restrained.

An unrestrained heart that sings for Jesus is the most lethal weapon God has. For that heart releases others.

It is like a prisoner with keys while the guard is asleep.

That unrestrained soul will freely flutter through the whole prison proclaiming release for all and there is nothing that the detention boss will be able to do about it.

Because his keys have been stolen and his guards are asleep.

That released soul is certain to tell the rest where the keys are. And, that soul has been released for all eternity because Satan has no power to take the keys from those for whom they have been left.

When your dad leaves the house key on the table, you come along and pick it up.

Once it is in your pocket, that's it, game over, Satan looses.

Doors are open.

No more locked doors for you!

Chapter VI

Anointing

In this mart, there are lots of exchanges, trade offs. We down what we have, and get what we never thought possible.

Anointing

Often times, we think anointing is given to a select group of Christians who get a special gift from God. We think of it like a touch by a fairy's wand. They have told us that, "God called me." We think that we need a burning bush or a Holy visitation to be anointed.

This is not true. There is anointing waiting for each of God's Children who seek him, and are obedient to His words. To be anointed means that we have been set apart for a specific purpose. God has a purpose for each of us; a job in His Kingdom.

Only, most of the time, we are the last ones to figure out what it is.

He says that we are to love him with all our heart, soul, and strength. We first learn to love Him, then, as we get our mind into the Scriptures, we start to be changed. Our soul starts to love Him. It is funny how our feet always follow our heart and soul.

I picture it as a walk. It is like we walk from one green field to another. One field could be of oats and the other of rye grass. We are walking along through the fields.

Using the field analogy, the first field is grown from oat seeds. The oat seeds symbolize the seeds of thinking.

This field is filled with the way that we have been taught since we were small. We have built our ideas around these seeds of thought.

An example of the thinking that we were raised on might be, "Pull yourself up by your own bootstraps." From this idea we press on to build our thinking. We might refuse to as for help when we actually need it. We put ourselves through school and don't depend on others when we should.

The first field is grown from ideas implanted by our parents, our schooling, and our Church. Anyone that is around us influences us. The television is a large influence in growing seeds of this first field.

To continue with the analogy, we press on with our walk and move into the next field; the rye field. We have a change of heart and realize that God may have some ideas he would like to share with us. So, we begin to read the Bible. When we do, our thinking starts to change. As in the analogy, the seeds change from oats to rye. The seeds of the Word of God start to grow in our minds.

Perhaps, we learn the verse that says, "trust in the Lord with all your heart. Do not depend on your own insight..." We start to change our ways of thinking about dependence on God. At this point, we have left the field of oats and entered into the field of the rye grass; we have begun to walk into the anointing that God has already laid out for us.

We see those with 'an incredible anointing'. Actually, they are just further into the rye grass field. These have allowed their minds to be transformed with the seeds of the Word and their feet to walk in obedience further into the field that God has planned for them.

Become Empty

When we enter the Kingdom of God we become washed from our sins. Then, we become anointed. To become anointed is to be set apart for a specific purpose and given a direction within that purpose. It is a blessing of inheritance given by the Father as He releases jobs within the Kingdom.

God is like a container that fills us up. We must come to Him with openness to be ready for Him to fill us up. We have to empty ourselves of what we are holding onto in order to have empty hands to do whatever He asks us to do.

If our hands are already full of doing what we think that we are supposed to be doing, then we will not be available to do what He asks. He is the beaker that holds all that we need for the service He wants to put us into. He overflows to us.

The Holy Spirit provides guidance to us. When He fills us, the anointing comes as part of the package. We are to become little cups, having been poured into by Him, we, then are poured out to others.

Our cup is filled with what ever the Lord has given us to do the assignment He desires within his Kingdom. Whatever we hold in our hand is what He wants to use for His purposes. It is a cup, not a glass because it must have a 'handle' that is held by God.

When we learn to hear His voice and walk in obedience to it, the oil of His joy will flow into our cup. Then, there reaches a point when our cup is full to overflowing, and starts to overfill. If this cup, this anointing, is near others, then it spills over to them. It is then that we will walk in the reason that we were made. Our heart begins to sing. Others notice, believe me, I know.

Before I entered my own rye field, I had never written a single paper. I had not written a poem or a story that I would be willing to let others read. I had no journal. But, as I began to walk into the rye field, He had prepared for me, I was moved by the Holy Spirit to begin to write. Because I pray, He responded to me with learning principles for prayer. All I did was to write them down. I never knew that it was to be a book. He did not tell me that part for two years into my journaling. I think that I would have been too scared to continue if I would have realized how far into the rye field He was to take me.

I consider my life as a book, not that I have written several books. This is an overflow to what He teaches me. My cup was filled, then, overflowed onto the paper.

Share

The anointing is meant to be shared with others, so that God will be praised. It is meant to be our tithe to the Body of Christ. A perpetual joy comes, as we walk with His anointing, in His presence.

There is an anointing waiting for each of us. He has placed a flask of oil on the table of His presence right next to the bread.

When we ask the Holy Spirit to come into our lives, He anoints our head with His oil like a priest. It is like oil to dry skin. It is then, that we will begin to understand His love for us because it is the Holy Spirit that brings us understanding of the things of God. His love goes straight to our heart to become the foundation and strength of the anointing.

Mary Anoints and is Anointed

The oil is like a flask that must be broken and opened to be used. It comes with a cost to the one who has it. Mary anointed the feet of Jesus before she was anointed. She demonstrated from her heart emotional involvement. She wept. She allowed her heart to be moved by His presence. When we get in the position where God uses us to help anoint of the feet of others, there is a fragrance released.

Mary, used her hair to wipe the oil off of His feet. Each strand of our covering needs to be washed in the presence of the Savior. Just as she wiped his feet with her crown, her hair, it brushed his feet as it flowed down.

We need to pour out what we value most and let Him anoint it. He will purify our flow if we are willing to turn it over to him. All we value, we put it at the feet of Jesus and let it be anointed for His service. When we do this, we let our covering be His covering. What comes out of our head, (our hair) should be put to the test. We bring it into His presence with tears and anointing. What falls onto our shoulders, we lay at his feet. Take it all to Him.

As she anointed Him with tears and inner cleansing, bringing her gift, He anointed her because of her position and place at His feet. She was humble and obedient. She expended herself. She was open and broken before Him, first, then others. She didn't care for others, but set her mind to do what was right. She was anointed because she purposefully brought her oil to the feet of Jesus. She worshipped Him with her adornment. Her union with Jesus was planned. She knew who He was and took her relationship with Him personal. I am sure that she had often sat at His feet. She knew that these were the feet of God. She knew His purpose for coming to the earth was to die for Her sins. His feet were to be anointed because they were to carry out the walk to fulfill the plan for salvation. It was His feet that gave Him the ability to walk in the right direction.

The Lord draws people using His love as a banner. We are the ones to do the drawing as His hand is upon us. We are the signs, the banners that point the way to Him.

Genesis 8.11, Deuteronomy 14.23, Nehemiah 8, Esther 9.22, Job 33.26, Psalms 4.7, 28.7, 45.7, 71,104, 133, Isaiah 12.3, 56, 60, 61,65, Jeremiah 11.16, Zechariah 4.3, Luke 10.21, John 3.29, 15,16,17, Hebrews 1.9, I Peter 1.8, Romans 11, Galatians 4,5, James 3.12.

Chocolate Pad

There is a pad in the box. I don't think my brother knows about it, because He thinks my sister needs Jesus. But, the real problem is that he is stuck in his own thinking. He built a Jesus Box and filled it with his own beliefs, carefully selected from his favorite books and lectures. But, when he carefully aligned his views of the sweetness of God, he forgot to put the paper in. It's the paper that pads the chocolates top and bottom to keep them from slipping around in the box. In this writing, the paper represents God's presence. Because when we formulate beliefs, theories, and ideologies about who God is, we need to ask Him. We need to sandwich all the teaching that we receive between his presence. Front and back. As we take in the material from others and we encapsulate it into our own lives. She doesn't need Jesus. I know because I talked to her. She believes the apostles creed and talks to God daily incorporating His presence into her life. She asks him stuff, and obeys his word. But, the other guy thinks she needs Jesus, because he doesn't see her going to church or reading the Bible. So, do they have the same Jesus? You bet. There is only one Jesus. It is just that he doesn't recognize the way she relates to God because it is so different from the way he does. Who is wrong? Neither. I pray for her, she will read the Bible and go to Church. And, I pray for him that he will come to understand the presence of God on a daily basis.

More Candy Pads

You see, she, too, has a box. Hers doesn't have much in it. Pretty much papers. So, when he lifts her lid, that is all he sees. And, right now he does not understand just how important those papers are. But, hopefully, soon, he will. Because, with his box of chocolates, if it gets tipped sideways, they end up in a pile at one end. When adversity or sudden change comes to his world, he hasn't learned how to call on the presence of God for answers, but reaches into his box for a chocolate. His whole teaching has to be realigned to account for new information. During this time, there is a shuffle in his thinking and a stall in his ministry. Hopefully, soon, he will learn about the pad for his ministry. The one that keeps the teaching stabilized because it allows for continued change. The presence of God is what makes the Holy Spirit flow. To be a river, rather than lake. It allows for change along our path. He sees her without stability and she sees him as rigid. But, in reality, she flows and he is stagnant.

Trees

It is within God's plan for trees and plants to grow. Christians are called trees within the Kingdom of God. So, there are a lot of parallels between the forests and us. They are supposed to yield seed.

So are we. We are supposes to yield to know Him and plant the seed of His word. We are to bear fruit; the fruits of the Spirit. Each of us will bear fruit according to our kind. If we have fruits of love, joy, peace, patience, kindness and goodness, this is what we will share with others.

Seed is within the plant as it sucks nutrition from the soil. It grows roots in love then grows upward. Reaches upward; extends itself. This tree is supposed to reach out to God. We bear fruit with seed in it. The fruits of the Spirit are displayed within us into others lives contain the seeds of God. They are painted; displayed, brushed. God's word is the prompt to display His fruit.

He provides the seed. The seed is of His imperishable word; eternal seeds. We give others from the trees that are provided.

Then, we serve them. Through our flesh or through the Spirit of God that lives within us. When we serve Christ through our flesh, it is a stumbling block to others. It is as if we are giving them wax fruit. There are no seeds. It only looks like fruit. When they eat it, there is no nourishment. This type of fruit has no eternal value to them. When we learn to walk by the Spirit it prevents the flesh from running the show.

The trees of God are beautiful. They are food for the eyes. When the eyes of our heart are open, we can see the beauty displayed through the growth of God's people. It is the growth within the kingdom of God.

God's trees are good for food. They provide for us all the riches of God. He provides through His Holy Spirit, all of Himself within these trees if they give of their fruit.

It is like God has given us a tree called Life which has all sorts of fruits hanging on it. We come along with our basket and stand under Him. When we do, He fills our basket with His fruits. Then, we deliver the fruits to others within the basket that He has provided. The fruits are love, joy, peace, patience…etc. We bring His love in what ever basket He provides.

The gifts are the packaging of the fruit to others. We may ask God to give us one of the fruits. It starts to grow on our tree; our life. We may be growing 'love'. The package is how that fruit is given to others. Maybe we are jars; like jars that jelly can be put in. If we are jars, then it is like being a book writer. The fruit is opened at the readers' leisure to give them seeds to the Kingdom of God.

If we see fruit and ask God for it, He will graft it into our tree. We can mix plums and pears and oranges and apples and have them grow from the same root; the love of God. Then we will have fruit in every season. We will be ready in every season to present the gospel to others.

God plants the seeds because He is the one that tends our soul. We entrust ourselves to Him and He waters and feeds us. We raise our arms to Him and open our branches to praise Him. He reigns over us. He snows on us with forgiveness. He shines His Son light into our hearts.

The trees of God's garden are for anyone to eat from freely. There is no cost for His fruit. Freely we have been given, freely we are to give. We don't pick fruit from our branches for others. God is the one who gives to others. We need to keep our branches in a position of adoration to God. Occasionally, someone may shake our tree. Our world may be shaken by issues. What will happen if we are firmly rooted in the love of Christ is that our fruit will fall on the person's head. (Gen 3.15) If they re the enemy of God's Kingdom, then they will become wounded by Him, by His seed. If they are a friend of God, they will know when to reach their hands upward toward Him and catch the fruit as it falls. It is positional.

What is the tree of the Knowledge of Good and Evil?

To know good and evil is to become aware of both good and evil, not just one side. Adam and Eve had their eyes opened to see that they were under the protection of God's love. Before they ate from the tree, they were not aware that they were under the umbrella of love and protection.

When they became disobedient, they walked out from under the umbrella of protection. Then they became exposed to the elements of whether. Weather or not to follow God's voice or the Serpent's voice. His voice prompted them to doubt God's voice. The doubt was the seed that planted the tree that produced the fruit of disobedience to God.

The disobedience caused the separation of the two trees because the flesh is at enmity with the Spirit. They caused the separation of flesh and spirit and soul when they followed their own flesh (desire to eat). It led their soul into lust. They forgot about their spirit. They went upside down.

The trees of Satan grow downside up. From earth up. God's trees grow from up side to down. From heaven to earth. They are led by the Spirit which leads the soul, which leads the flesh. Satan's trees are from themselves to others. You to me. What do you have for me? What can you do for me? It looks for others to love him. It desires to be loved first. Reaches within for resources. Pulls things out of the air.

The two trees are at enmity and they could not grow in the same garden. We need to plant ourselves within the stream of the counsel of God. He will provide us with non stop information on how to live. We will become aware of the seasons. He trims us back; pulls us in and out of a lot of activities to make us produce more fruit when the season is right. He waters us with a constant supply of His presence when our roots are planted in a desire to grow in His love.

Genesis 1, 2,3, Psalms 1.3, Proverbs 3, Song of Solomon 8, Jeremiah 17.8, Micah 4.4, Isaiah 61.3, Amos 2.9, John 9.8,37, Luke 19.4, Galatians 5.22, 6.8 Jude 12, Revelation 2.7, 22.2.

On Cue

When you play a piano, you press harder on the keys to make the sound louder. God wants us to press Him. He says if we press Him, He presses back. When we play the heart strings of God, it puts everybody on cue. When we each learn our key, the orchestra will play in harmony. Just like each of us are the keys on the piano, we play a different tone. But, when we are in harmony, and on cue, there will be a complete song.

146

Be Sifted

Flour is sifted to remove the Lumps. Make it soft and ready to mix with other ingredients. We are sifted through the fingers of God to be put into a cup. To be measured out to others to become a delicate dessert for the children.

Drive a Peg

God is looking for tent pegs to hold up the ropes for the tent of His presence. A tent peg is a stake that is driven into the ground around which a rope can be tied. It holds up something much bigger than itself by virtue of its position.

God want us to drive the tent pegs in the Kingdom of God. We are to push the nails that are driven through the purposes of Jesus. We need to become aligned with His purposes for coming to the earth. God coming in the flesh was to provide a sacrifice for our sins through the blood of Jesus. It is 'through' His flesh that we have life. Because Jesus gave His life, we can have life.

It is His bittersweet plan to heal our suffering by His suffering. This is the only way He can offer us all of the blessings that are held within His Kingdom. Any purpose that is put into our hand and 'nailed to the cross' becomes like a peg to hang things on.

We must push the nail 'purpose' through using the blood of Jesus as the thing that makes the covenant complete. The blood of Jesus, His sacrifice on the cross, is what all of the Salvation package is 'through'. We must be willing to face the cross, the spilling of his blood, for the purpose of our own salvation, to be able to push through whatever purpose He has for us within His Kingdom. All of the purposes hang on His provision.

But now for a brief moment grace has been shown from the Lord our God, to leave us an escaped remnant and to give us a peg in His holy place that our God may enlighten our eyes and grant us a little reviving in our bondage. (Ezra 9:8)

A nail is used to hang stuff on. In the garage we hang tools on them. In the house we hang the things that adorn the house. God wants to show us how to hang the things that adorn his house; the Church. He wants to show us how to hang extraordinary things on three extraordinary nails.

Authorized Candy Wrapper

Dream:

My Father owned a candy store by the sea. I was an authorized wrapper, but had no credentials given to me from the outside schools. We go to a church to pray to God.

Something is planted. A piece of heavy equipment comes in to help. It is like a back hoe. Water is spilled from the back of the sanctuary. It is going to flow from the back into the sanctuary. They use the bucket on the backhoe to gather the water and scoop it out. They bring in something powerful, first to plant, then to control the flow of the Holy Spirit.

We leave to get out of the way. I need a ride to the next place. It's late. I go to a place. I think maybe I'll ask someone for a ride, then, I learn that the bus will be by anytime. I already have enough money, so I just need to find the ticket counter. I had raised some money for the school children, but it wasn't enough. So I was being sent to the big city, to the capital (Wash DC) to get more. A bigger audience, a bigger picture. The white house.

Interpretation:

God has placed His stamp of approval me, like a box of chocolates. I do not need credentials from schools here on earth. He has set His seal on me and given me His authorization to share His sweetness with others. I am the package that He has provided to share sweet things with His people. It is by my sharing with them how to see Him for themselves apart from others telling them. He wants to speak to them, Himself. He wants to teach them to listen to His voice.

The sweetness of God is shared through His church. He wants us to become people of prayer joined together to seek His face. He will plant His church. It is to be started with His love, His sweetness. He wants to bring His heaviness, His Holy Glory into the Church. He comes to us through the open doors of hearts responding to His voice.

He does not come from those in front, but in back, willing to serve Him.

In the dream the Glory of God brought through the baptism of the Holy Spirit is spilled onto the people, His way, not the way that the leaders want it. They want to control, but He wants to control His way. When they try to remove the Holy Spirit from the Church, it is as if one would remove water with buckets or a back hoe. God's water continues to flow from a spring that wells up in the back of the building.

One of the messages of this dream is that we need to get out of the way when the Spirit flows. In the dream, I back out the door. I make sure that they don't think I am the cause. I take no credit for the movement of God. It is Him, not me.

God wants us to use the spiritual gifts He has provided for leading. We already have enough provision for His purposes, but we need to find the ticket counter. It is a place where we can cash in the gifts God has given us, for what will take us to the place He wants us to go. There is an exchange that needs to happen.

The gifts of the Spirit are not merely to encourage, but give us direction, as well. We need to go to the table of His presence and meet Him with them there. He is the ticket counter. It is like an exchange counter, where He trades in the gift for direction. For example, He gives the gift of interpretation of tongues, when we ask.

I have asked and received this gift. I believe that God will give this gift to anyone who asks for it. Paul, says that He would rather speak a few words that others understand, then a lot of words that nobody understands. If we are to interpret God's word for others, we must ask for the gift of interpretation.

Let me demonstrate the interaction of the gifts along with interpretation; Last week when I was at work, I ended up in the hall of the Emergency Room along side of a woman.

Within a few minutes, she learned that I am into dreams. She told me her dream. In her dream, she goes to a lovely city, full of wonderful things to buy. While she is there she wants to buy some of the things, but she has no money. She does not even have enough to get home, for she cannot ride the bus.

So, I asked her, "Is there something that you want, that you do not have?"

"Yes," She replied, "My sister has a wonderful relationship with God. I want one, but I do not know how to get it."

So, I responded, "I think that what you need is not money. You think that you need money. But, usually, you cannot ride a bus with money. You need a token."

She became excited, because she realized that was her problem. I told her that what she was missing was the Holy Spirit. Then, I invited her to pray with me for the baptism of the Holy Spirit. She agreed.

And, there in the middle of the Emergency Room hall we prayed. She said three words and I said three words. She said, "Holy Spirit, Come."

And, I said three words in tongues. I say them very slowly for those I pray over, and interpret each word. So, I grabbed a small piece of paper and jotted down the three words in tongues. Then, under them I wrote the interpretation of the three words.

I would not let her see the words until I was finished. I told her, "By this, you will know that it is God who is speaking to you. For these words come with the power of His voice. You will know when I tell you."

Then, I gave her the words. They were something like, "Daughter, I have released My Kingdom to you."

She started to cry. And I left. I simply walked out of the Emergency Room. For, it was the end of my shift.

But, I cried as well. All the way home. For, in a few minutes God had used me to interpret her dream, lead her to the Holy Spirit, pray over her in tongues, interpret the tongues, and walk out, leaving the glory to Him. I never told her my name.

We will do well to pray for the gift of interpretation. It is very powerful for individuals to know what God is saying as we speak in tongues.

Then, practice slowing down, and allowing the interpretation time to catch up because, just like any other language, the interpreter can only interpret as fast as the brain can handle. And, if you are the one speaking in tongues, you also need time to speak the interpretation. You have to be two people. So, we need to slow down. God's word is powerful. It does not take much to change lives. All of the titles of the books I have written are in tongues with the interpretations given. I make no excuse, because all who read them, and read the underscore, know that is what it means.

Another message of the dream is that the Lord wants more white interpretation of His word. Increased purity is closer to the center of His Kingdom. He desires increased purity in vision to help clear up what He is saying. With increased purity, we will be given more responsibility. God is faithful to send us His message, we need to become faithful to receive them.

Authorized Wrapper

We have God's stamp of approval to share with others His goodness when He has wrapped Himself around us, and when we have wrapped ourselves around Him. He provides the box and the bow. We hand it to others.

Unclaimed Packages

Like stacks of mail at the post office, I am looking over the vast amount of information that no one pushes up from that sea.
Going to where I am and seeing Me as I truly am.
Asking Me who I am.
They have asked everybody but Me.
The unclaimed mail is still there.
Letters to My children.
Like love letters, I send them, yet they remain unclaimed, like letters marked 'return to sender.'
They leave them there.
Information About Me, like unclaimed baggage packages unaccounted for at the Post Office.
I send messages, but, they are not opened.
Three quarters of the earth is sea.

Fun Learning

I'm trying to forward the Kingdom of God. They are at the place where they teach them to fly. I know how. I am experienced and have been for a lot of years. I am comfortable there and have fun midst others who are new at it. Somebody tries to put a damper on my fun with the boys and I don't let him. We're just having a good time. There's fun on the surface but serious under tones to all. They really are learning from me.

Locked Fun

Dream:

I'm at an amusement park. I leave and my Mother tells me to go back. We left something there.

There is fun locked in the foundation.

Interpretation:

God wants us to have fun. He is the Father of delight. The closer we come to Him, the more fun-loving we will become. He wants to take us for rides that provide us with maximum thrills.

The interpretation of dreams is very fun. It shows the humor of God. He loves riddles. He loves the effort that we put into figuring them out. He wants to be the center of fun, too. Why not?

Often, we have an image of a stern God who is sitting on a stone throne with a long robe on. He wants to replace that image of Himself with one that is true. I believe that if He was to take us to the carnival, He would buy us the twenty pack of tickets and ride the rides with us. This Father smiles and laughs out loud. He invented emotion and has all of it.

The message of the dream is that we have left the amusement area of God's world. We have left the 'fun' part of God behind. We have separated that aspect of Him without His permission. He does not want to be serious all of the time. He wants to love us delightfully, in every way.

Joy and Delight

Joy and delight, delight and glee.
In Me with you and you with Me.

Miracles

The Dream:

I am with my friends and a 'talent search' company came along. They do shows on 'miracles'. Together, they pressure me to audition.

I was given some salt and a cup of water and told to, "Sprinkle the water and salt on the ground."

The ground was desert. I was enthusiastic and started to pour the water and sprinkle. Where ever I poured the water and sprinkled the salt peanut plants came up. They grew before my eyes and became mature. Before I realized it, I was so excited that I was dancing and singing and sprinkling everywhere. I even went to a patch of concrete and sprinkled and plants came up. I just knew that they would come up anywhere.. and they did right through the concrete. The cup never ran out of water and the salt never ran out.

After a while I stopped. And, only then, did I remember that I was supposed to be auditioning for a role. I had put more into the part than I realized. I forgot that people were watching. Then, I got worried because I knew that I was perfect for the role and they would want to sign me up. It was insecurity.

I knew that, in my heart, I had all that they needed for the part, only I would have to not look at the people on the sidelines. I would have to keep focused on the salt and water.

Interpretation:

The talent search company is the Father in Heaven. He has come to check on me to see what I have done with the talent that He has given me. (Matthew 25:14-30)

He is looking to see what we have done with the talents that He has given us. He needs stars in his show. He wants to show the world Himself. He shows himself through His reflection on us. We become stars that reflect His glory into darkness.

God has given us friends, the brothers and sisters in Christ to help us step into the role that we are to play within the Kingdom of God. When we encourage and elevate one another toward God's talent search, it promotes Him. One of the best ways that God can be recognized is through miracles. A miracle is like a power serge, by God, to right a situation that is wrong. What we have come to see as 'upright' gets turned over. When it gets turned over to God, then He makes it 'upright'. Only, then do we realize it was not right before. The sick are made well, the lost are brought home, and families are restored.

Often, we thought that we needed to endure sickness. We had come to accept having our children afar. We have went to counseling for broken families, rather than see them restored. A miracle happens when God steps in with His power and His word. The Spirit of might flows. We put on a show for others when our heart is to serve God. In the dream, I am given water in a cup. Jesus says that if we give a child a cup of water in His name it is as if He has given it. He provides the water to us. He gives us all things of Himself. We need to become willing to share Him with others. We did not pay for any of it, we have no need to hoard it.

The cup is filled with water. Water is the presence of God. He has put into my hand His presence. He has made Himself known to me. I make His presence known to others. He does not give His Spirit by measure; which means that when He comes, all of Him comes. Bring it on!

He gives me salt, as well. Salt is seasoning for food. Jesus, the Word is the food. The salt is for the food. God brings His Word in season to His people through our hand. When we step into what He has for us, He will use us to bring His Word in season with His presence. This combination opens the way for miracles. Plants grow through cement.

The plants are peanuts. Peanuts are not normal plants. They give nitrogen into the soil. It is a basic element that is essential for other plants to survive. Nitrogen is also a chemical that is used in explosions. It burns quietly when heated in air, but explodes when heated under pressure.

A Word from God in season combined with the presence of the Holy Spirit is like a peanut plant. It imparts nitrogen into the soil that makes us grow. It causes Holy Spirit explosions. We will 'burn' quietly in God's presence in our alone time with him, but when He places us under pressure; when He presses us with his issues, then it will cause an explosion.

When nitroglycerin is detonated it produces 10,000 x it's own volume in gas. There is unlimited potential in the kingdom of God when we are willing to audition for His talent search.

Matt 5.13-20, Mark 9.38-49, Luke 14:25-35, Ephesians 1, 2.

Dialysis

Dream:

We need dialysis. Join with each other and have dialysis. The flow is light.

Interpretation:

Dialysis filters the impurities out of the blood. It takes out the waste and purifies it. God wants to purify us. He wants to purify the flow from us. The flow of the Holy Spirit needs to become pure. We are full of waste products. We are retaining things that we need to let go of.

There are things in our lives that we should not be hanging onto. There are things that are circulating in our body that shouldn't be. There are things that are a waste and need to be gone.

What are we doing that we are a waste? A waste is something that is of no eternal purpose. It is taking up the space where something productive belongs. If we have ideas that are not from God, they are taking up the place where His ideas need to be.

God wants to purify us. To have dialysis, individuals are attached to a machine that puts a flow of water directly into their artery. The water is ordered by the physician to contain elements that will pull the bad elements from the body. Then there is a second line that removes the waste from the body. It runs into the sink and down the drain. God wants us to hook into Him; His line to us. He wants to become the flow into our heart. He is the physician that knows what we need and He has written the orders for us specially designed to take the waste and remove it from us. Everything we need is in the solution of the flow. God will become our solution with His flow when we open up to Him. There needs to be an 'in flow' and an 'out flow'.

We need to ask God to come and change us; make us into what He wants us to be. Then, we need to open ourselves up to let go of what ever He tells us to. There are things in our lives that we have been hanging onto. He will come to us and tell us what needs to done away with. If someone is connected to dialysis, He cannot have an inflow without an outflow. *The flow is light.* God's word brings light to us. The light reveals things that have been hidden in the dark places of our heart. When His word reveals things that need to be confessed, we need to deal with them. For, when we confess our sins to God that we receive healing and find grace to help in a time of need.

155

Temperamental Tempest

Temperamental tempest is a storm with a mighty variable personality.

You never know when it's going to suddenly storm.

Blowing wind, rain, mighty thunder.

Crashing rain. Run for cover.

Caused by instabilities in the atmospheric pressures.

Hot meets cold, up meets down and causes severe updrafts and down drafts.

Air lifts and drops.

Tempest. Wind.

You really can tell when its coming, though.

There's a quietness and a sucking back.

Like a pulling back, a sudden quietness, a lack in activity. Then, all of a sudden, all hell breaks loose.

The enemy has fired on you with evil winds.

Spiraling sucking winds meant to destroy, take out stuff you have built. The blowing will take out anything not founded on the love of God.

Love Check. Like an oil check in the car.

To those in active service for God, it should be routine.

Just like the afternoon thunder storms in a tropical climate.

So, we prepare, gird up the loins of your mind to focus on the love of Christ and His blood sacrifice for us.

That's all. Avoid confrontations on religion and theology, doctrines and History.

Focus on Him, the Giver of Life, master of Peace amidst the storm.

He will encase us in His love amidst the mess.

Waft of Righteousness

When the trees are healthy the forest smells good. A Christian who walks with righteousness through Jesus, put out a waft of delightful aura everywhere he walks. *Lord, teach us to be your fragrances. One that causes others to pause, inhale and seek to see where it comes from.*

Annulment from the World

I want an annulment, please, dear Lord. A pause. A divorce from someone I didn't mean to wed. I had no idea of the long term complications, and now I want out. Annul my formal relationship with this world, please, Lord. And allow me to be free to marry Jesus. Then, we can have a decent wedding in the church and invite all our friends. They will see our love and commitment, unity and responsibility. We will have oodles of spiritual children. Birth visions and dreams, one after another and raise them up to the honor of God, our Father. I never meant to marry this world, Dear Lord.

Forgive me, please. I want to stop being unfaithful and become whole hearted in my commitment to my new love. Release me, please. Let me go. Erase the commitments I have declared true in the past. Because I have found the truth. I am done philandering. I want to settle down and spend some time with an eternal love, Jesus. His cords of love have wrapped my heart. The love songs he has sung to me have melted me in a place I never knew existed. So, I am enthralled, and know I can never go back to my old lover. But, still, I want to make it legal. So, Lord, please release me from the standards of commitment to the world, and attach me to Yours. Amen.

Safe Harbor

Once you knew me. Eternal God. Twice you loved me. Before I was born and after. Enveloped in your love, surrounded by Your righteousness, bathed in Your forgiveness, coated with grace, I sail into Your safe harbor under the wind of the Holy Spirit.

Walk into the Steps

Dream:

Walk into the steps. Go toward.

Interpretation:

When we pray into the will of God, then we can pray with faith that it will happen. If we ask God what His will is, then pray 'into' that perfect will, then we are guaranteed victory. We need to walk toward him. He is calling out to us.

When we ask Him something, we need to wait on Him for the answer. Then have a pad and pen ready to copy it. Sometimes it will not make sense right then. But, we can always take it back to Him again and again for clarification. He will be true to answer us.

Also, maybe He doesn't want to reveal all of the steps in the process at this time, for what He is doing. He wants us to step out in faith with the information that He gives us. He wants us to go toward the answer.

Sometimes, when He gives an answer, it is not the final answer. There are several steps in-between that must be done first to get there. He may be sending us in a specific direction for another purpose.

Perhaps he tells us to go to a Church meeting at a different Church. At first, He tells the purpose. Then, when we go, we learn that there are several other purposes for us being there. He just needed to get us there in the first place. We simply, need to start walking and trust that He knows the plans.

Fast Train

Let the fasting begin like runners on a line start at the shot of a gun and finish at the ribbon. Run the race with endurance, go the mile. Eat up the track, instead of food. For you are what you eat. Become a fast train on the track to the miracles of God's Kingdom. It's the Am Track. The God I AM track. Climb aboard, and take a seat, Look out the window God has provided. Let Him conduct the show.

Release the Singers

Since we are surrounded by so great a cloud of witnesses, let us lay aside every weight and sin that clings so closely and run with perseverance the race that is set before us; looking to Jesus the author and perfecter of our faith...

The race is easier to run without weights. Send it to Jesus. He paid the price. He's the author and the perfecter of our faith walk. It's about getting our heart to sing.

Our heart can't sing with Jesus' heart if it wearing handcuffs. It needs to be released first. Released to praise. Our praise is being held by things unknown to our present mind. By his stripes we are healed. He was beat so that we won't be.

How? Our wounds have healed over with scar tissue. They are crusted over; filled with granulation tissue. We see through scales. Our scales need to fall from our eyes.

Our own weights on our own scales. Like A big steel door on a penitentiary. When we align ourselves with his mold.

Lock and key. Then the door will open with a rumble and a crash. He doesn't want to make us over, but fit to us.

Every nook and cranny. Free the singers. Its the 40 stripes. They encircled his whole body.

He doesn't release the weights, we let go. His arms are already extended to take them.

Interactive Food

Even picky eaters like marshmallows
because they are fun.
They are interactive food.
The sugar reacts with the flame.
Sweetness and passion.
Mellows and fire from within.
Desire and longing.
Reverence and zeal.

Prayer of Passing Trains

It is an error to presume to know where another person's heart is when we pray with him. Only God knows hearts.

Lord, help us to get our heart and our lips moving in the same direction.

The reason we cannot see into other's hearts is that there is too much glass between. It is like we are in a train looking out our window. We see the world through the window of our soul.

Then, another train passes with someone else in it. That person looks out their window at you. If the angle is just right, maybe your gaze will match. But, if it is not, you will never see one another at all. Now, suppose both trains stop on the track.

You stop in your tracks and spend time with someone. Still, you have all those windows. Are they clean? Can you keep from focusing on the dead bugs and splatters on the windows to focus on each other. Not hardly.

That is why when we pray with another, we must both focus on God, who is in our car. We can see His face plainly and He sees ours. Then, as the two trains pass, it does not matter how much we interacted as long as our relationship drew us closer to God.

Our purpose in prayer is to get closer to God, to know His heart and learn His ways for us. We must have the same purpose for others.

Sweet Times

There is sweet times of redemption for God's people. Cookies and milk after school given by our mother, Wisdom. Presence and sweetness after our training. Good idea. We need more classes to end this way.

He pushes The Purpose

Dream:

We have to see the purpose before we can see the presence. He pushes you into the presence by direction.

Interpretation:

We cannot get into the presence of God without His direction. God is Holy and we are pretty far from it. But, He has provided hope to us. The Holy Spirit has been working in our lives since before we were born to coax us toward God.

God has always purposed to be friends with us. He has always wanted to become our intimate soul mate. We could never drag Him onto our side of the tracks because of our sinfulness, but in His love for us, He has provided a way to lift us to his side. His Holy Side.

The purposes of God are built on His Word. We can stand firm on His Word; His promises. The plans of God were sealed when Jesus rose from the dead and ascended into heaven. He has given us the Holy Spirit to remind us of the plans and help guide us to fulfill our part in building the Kingdom. We tap into the mind of God because of His interpreter, the Holy Spirit.

He helps us to understand God's purposes and His ways. He explains the mysteries to us. Then, to top it off, He provides the power to bring those plans into fulfillment within our lives. He unites His purpose with His plans into fulfillment according to His power flowing through us as we open our heart up to Him.

God has an intended purpose for each of us. He has planned for us to have a place within the building of the Church. His mission will thread through our ministry, our teaching and our way of life. Our ways will be His ways, not our own.

God purposes in His heart, then, develops the plans. His purposes will succeed. One of His purposes is to remove the yoke of Satan from his people. He exposes the hidden desires of the enemy and exposes his plans for us.

The Lord wants to remove the burdens that have been placed on us and give us freedom. Set us free. His purpose is to give us all of His riches that are held within His Kingdom available through Jesus Christ.

No one can turn back the hand of God when it is stretched out.

When we walk into this plan, we will only be met with 'yes'. There are no closed doors when we follow God's plan and His voice.

When God has a purpose to fulfill, He will call on someone who will do it. He has given us the Spirit of Wisdom to help direct us into the building of His Kingdom. When we do not seek His counsel, then our plans will fall. But, when we seek His purposes, He will rescue us His way, His direction. He won't drop us there. He will continue to lead us through the rescue. His voice is alive; it is active. His word flows.

We can tap into Him any time we want and He will give us direction. He looks for those who will do what He says when He says it, to who He needs the message to go to.

It is like a Father calling to His children from across the park. He calls us to help someone in need. Often, we don't know why we come when He calls. This is why we need to be in constant communication with Him. For, when He calls, and we come, He is faithful to tell us why, and we help to fulfill His purposes.

Nehemiah 8.4, Job 17.11, 33.17, Proverbs 15, 20, Isaiah 14.24-27, 46.11, II Corinthians 1.17, 9.11, Ephesians 1, 3, 2 Timothy 1.9, 3.10.

Chalupa Walk

Chalupas love to walk. They don't own cars or sled dogs or motorcycles, or horses. They are a people who have their own trails and love to walk on them: one village to the next ,to the market and back. Walk, walk, walk, walk, walk, walk, walk. Take a lesson. Sometimes we are lazy. We want to get into someone else's wagon and have them drive us around instead of having our own walk with Jesus. There is something to be said for the relationship of the moccasins with the soil. The movement of the feet along the path, kicking up dirt, meeting wild life along the way, and picking berries. For, when we walk on our own trail with Jesus, the relationship becomes more personal because I'm convinced He was a Chalupa.

162

Core of the Fruit

There
is an
ice chest in the back of the
Van. It is full of fruit for the kids.
The ice chest has apples in it for others.
Don't think that you are going to give them yours.
I have called you to take the lid off the ice chest that
Holds the picnic for My Children.
They must let Me drive,
give Me control,
then move to the
Rear of the bus. We are
covered with the love and wisdom of our Father.
He will blanket us in His provisions, as we come to Him.
The chest in the back of the bus, is God's chest, His
heart. We need to go to Him, open his chest, and
seek the fruits of the Holy Spirit for our
road trip. Then, go to the core.

The walk

Dream:

We were in a house. There were 3 bedrooms. All 3 daughters were together, so I let them decide which bed to sleep in.(My daughters, Stephanie, Esther, and me)

My eldest chose the large double bed. It was big, but there was a corner missing. She put the games away. My second daughter has the twins. I went to the master suite. It was a beautiful room with a king size bed. There were doors that opened to a rose garden. White lace sheer curtains danced with the breeze from the large open windows that overlooked the garden.

It's not about sharing your faith with others, it's about the walk.

Interpretation:

This dream is multifaceted. At the time I had the dream, my eldest daughter was living out of the state and not in touch with the rest of the family very much. I asked God about the bed she was sleeping in, and He instructed me. He said that although she was cutting corners, she was ready to put the games in her life, away. I prayed for Him to help her to put the games away and get things straight.

The next day, she called me to inform me that she was leaving the state and returning home to go to college. She was done wandering ready to enroll in school. In essence, she was ready to stop cutting corners and put the games away, beginning to get serious in life.

I will be curious to see if my youngest daughter has twins, as she is engaged to a man who is a twin, himself. I have recommended to her, that when she is ready to have children, she probably better gear up for twins.

So, this dream had an immediate message for me to pray, and most likely, a prophecy about my other daughter's family. Then, so as not to waste words, God provided an additional meaning for the dream in order to teach me.

I would not go so far as to say that my daughters represent each of the types of relationships, but rather, the beds are what represents the words of the dream. It is about three walks. Like the three pigs, it is three ways to walk with the clear message of the dream ending up in the master's suite.

There are three ways of looking at intimacy with God. The bed that is a double bed is a walk that cuts corners. This individual plays games with God. She has fooled herself that she is being intimate with God, but she is really playing high level games.

There is not enough room in her bed for a second person; God. She likes to think that there is enough, room, but if you pull back the covers, the truth will be disclosed. She plays with God like it is a game. She cuts corners off of what God has for her. She doesn't treat sharing Christ with others seriously.

She may only be trying to get numbers to 'win' the game. "The one with the most souls on their card in the end wins." These individuals are those who raise themselves above those who need saving. The bed in the dream was very tall. It is from an elevated position.

The bedroom with the twin beds refers to a person who invites God into their life, then tries to reproduce themselves. Then they try to reproduce themselves after others and have them reproduce after them. It is spiritual cloning. The dream teaches that this is not a good plan for saving souls.

When we reflect God, it doesn't mean that we are a clone of Him. We maintain individuals, but we have spiritual qualities that allow us to have companionship with Him.

In the third bedroom, the daughter sleeps with the King. She chooses the Master suite. In this type of relationship, He cares for His daughter. There is a 'tending' like a husband. When we allow God to tend us like a gardener tends his plants, then, He will tell us every step of the way.

Then, as we do what we are supposed to do, others will notice our walk and ask us about it.

This will be a constant witness to all those around us. When we focus on our intimacy with Him, He will move us into position to share with others as a process of our walk. He wants to become our 'husband' and put us up in a place of resting with Him. He wants us to abide with Him at His house. It is His desire for us to enjoy His company and to become our ever present companion day and night.

No Sweetness

Sweet potatoes with marshmallow topping are served at Thanksgiving. Communion and love. If we see a ministry and there is no sweetness, gentle flow of the love God atop the root of His Word; avoid it. Run For cover, get out of the way. It is not His.

Stealing Uniforms

Dream:
I am with a friend. We are on an empty bus and he steals some clothes out of someone's bag. They belong to a tall basketball player and will never fit him, but he steals them anyway. I say nothing

Then, we go into a garage and hide in the upper storage area. We watch people come to the house for a party while we hide. After a while, I get hungry and climb down from the garage. I go to the house where there are people having a party. The lady who is running the wedding ceremony comes to me and tells me that I have a place of honor at a table that is waiting. They have been waiting for me. Everything is set, all the arrangements have been made and it is free to me.

Interpretation:
We are on an empty bus. It is a means of transporting a lot of people to the same place. There are several seats where each person sits in their own seat while the driver takes them all to one place. Our movement toward Heaven is like we are on a bus. The Church should be moving together in the same direction. Each of us should assume the position that God as assigned to us. Then, we take our seats, look toward the front and leave the driving to God.

In the dream, the bus is empty because we are not taking our proper places using the transportation He has provided for us. This is a high school bus, like the one that transports a team. The Church is to work as a team with the unified goal of bringing as many to salvation and victory as possible.

Like a 'high' School basket ball team, God has uniforms for us to wear. He wants to be our tailor, to fit us for the attire that is perfect for us. It is the right size in every direction for the position that He has for us to play as part of the team.

On a football team, the kicker wears a different uniform than a fullback. He has special shoes whereas the fullback has special padding in certain places. They are each part of the team, but their attire is different.

God wants to give us special attire for the job within the Kingdom that He has prepared for us. If He wants us to be a writer, then He would dress us with provisions of computer skills, advanced education, and, perhaps, creativity in a certain direction. If He wants us to become an evangelist, He may give us a uniform with 'speaking skills' in our background. He steers us down the path His goals. We pay attention to His voice for the directives.

In the dream, we takes someone else's uniform. It does not fit. When we try to be someone that we are not, it does not fit. It won't fit our personality. It is not what we are meant to do within the Kingdom. It is just like a short person trying to wear a basketball uniform. Just because he puts on the uniform, does not mean that he will be able to play on the team in the same position that the other person plays.

We are not to follow in each other's footsteps, but in God's footsteps. Others can not teach us because our position is different. God has made us individual, just like snowflakes. None of us is alike. We may be similar, but not alike.

When we assume the position that God has intended for us, we become a tool to be used in His hand. In the dream, me and my friend become tools that are stored. We store tools when it is 'off season'. When we don't need the skis, we store them. When we don't need the rake or the hoe, we store it. Because me and my friend have taken a uniform that was not ours, it does not fit. When we put on attire that belongs to someone else, we will be out of place. We will feel out of season because we will be out of season. Nothing will feel right.

If our gifting is in the area of music, and we are trying to wear a 'uniform' of helping with Children's ministries, then it is like wearing a uniform that is not made for us. We will feel out of season because we will be out of touch with the season. It is not for us.

The true person will go into hiding behind the 'mask' of the other uniform. God cannot use us when we are not true to ourselves and Him.

When we do what God intends for us to do, it will satisfy us. We will not be satisfied and will continue to be hungry for what His intended purpose is for us until it happens. A race horse is not happy until he runs a race. A flower is not happy until he blooms. A preacher is not happy until he gives a sermon. A writer is not happy until she writes the message that God has placed on her heart… I know.

God places the hunger in our 'bosom' to fulfill the mission that He has planned for us. He will make us hungry to see that vision fulfilled. We will remain hungry, even though we may be very busy, when we are not doing His intended mission for us. He wants to satisfy us by bringing us into His house and feeding us with His vision and direction.

For me, in the dream, the party was already planned and the table was already set. I just needed to show up. I believe it is the same for every Child of God. He has a place prepared at his banquet, to feast on what His intended desire is for that person. There is a celebration when we finally figure out what it is… I can tell you.

Father, give us your vision for the true mission of our lives. We want to be invited to the party as a special guest. Amen

Deuteronomy 7.6-8, Ps 18, II Corinthians 5.11-21, I Peter 1.13-22, Ephesians 5:8-10.

Show and Tell, Words and Power

Sharing God's love is like Kindergarten. Remember when you returned from the weekend. Show and tell. I loved that part of the week. For, it was then that I told about some special time with my family and show them a memento that I had brought to prove that I was actually there. The Kingdom of God is supposed to be like show And tell. We should, not only tell them about Him, but show them. Demonstrate His power. Allow His love to flow through in our speech and our actions. For, when we show and tell, then, the whole of God comes through. The disciples knew how. For Paul says that he set his mind to preach The gospel, not merely with words but with action, thereby proving it to be true. If the gospel is true, then it will prove true. We should be able to Show and tell. Not only tell them about the power of God, but show them. Demonstrate His loving kindness through the gifts of the Holy Spirit as they flow through us.

Chapter VII

Share God's Heart

Through the Spirit of Life we have been given freedom to live in
this world, serving God with our hearts, not our hands.
Heart service.

Fire Screen

Dream:
A fire screen decorated with birds and leaves.

Interpretation:
Fire screen is a screen that sits on the hearth in front of the fire.
It is decorative and protective. It looks nice when there is no fire in
the fire place. When there is a fire, it protects people from the sparks
burning the house down. As the fire burns hotter, the screen is more
important to keep the hot ash from burning the surrounding area.

Just as the fire screen is a mesh of wire, it is similar to a message
system that brings messages from the fire of God to us. It symbolizes
the network of wire.

The Holy Spirit speaks to us. He brings us messages from God.
These messages are sent into our mind forming a panel in a window to
Heaven. This 'panel' separates the fire of God (the passionate love of
God) for His people as they sit at His altar hearth. Dreams are shown
on the screen of our mind. Our minds become the screen that the
pictures are shown on. They provide a window for God to talk to us.

We must set our face like a flint and enter into His light and heat by
placing ourselves at His altar hearth. We put ourselves in His presence
there.

When we do this, He ignites us with His fire. His presence has causes us to become aflame with His passion. He ignites us with His messages that he places on the screen of our mind.

Just as a screen is both decorative and protective there are similarities to its use there as well. God wants not only to adorn us, but to protect us. He desires that we listen to His 'wire mesh' and reflect His light to protect the ash form getting on others. As Children being raised in His presence, we are to absorb the ash. The residue from the burning; refining our lives and not allow that residue to overflow to others. As we become refined by Him, we need to be careful not to spill ash on others in the room.

Give the ash back to God. Ash is mortal remains that are burned; i.e. flesh. When we sacrifice ourselves to God, laying ourselves on the altar, he burns away the fleshly desires.

As we become more spiritual, we need to be careful not to brag about our spirituality. This is flipping ash on others in the room. We see ourselves becoming more pure, so we think that others are less pure. Well, they are, but it is not our job to tell them so. It is God's job.

The altar in the Old Testament is the table that is before the Lord where the bread of presence sits. We are to build an altar to the Lord; to heat up our relationship with him. The altar is a place to present a gift to God. Not a place to bring anything we may have against another. It is only a place for us and God to build a personal relationship.

I think of it as lounging in the living room in front of the fireplace with the Savior.

When we come to God and desire a relationship with Him, there must be an altar. We cannot have a relationship with God without his presence. Otherwise, it is just one-sided. We ask Him to teach us to learn to fear Him and Love Him. Then, we ask Him to help us become obedient from a pure heart. With His help, we can learn how to commune with Him.

He will bring us to the place where He dwells. We set our faces like a flint and allow His words to ignite fire in our lives. When we have become enveloped in that personal relationship with Him and keenly aware of His presence on a daily basis, then the fire of God will come down and ignite the sacrifice. It is praise and obedience to His word that He desires. When the fire of God comes down, it will burn up the flesh (our fleshly desires), the wood (words not from God) the representation of your own self, your own footing, and our own water (outflow that is not from God).

In Exodus Moses built an altar when they won the battle against the Amalekites. He called it 'The Lord is my banner'. For hands were lifted to the throne of the Lord.

Moses went to the top of the hill and held up his hands with the staff of the Lord. Moses' staff was a stick, but a staff can also be the 'stay' of our life, our bread. Jesus said that He is the bread. He has placed His presence within our reach through His sacrifice on the cross. The bread of God is in ours hands. When God gives us His word, we need to give it back as a sacrifice to Him. We should prayer holding it up to Him.

We are careful that we do not sacrifice things that cost us nothing. Something that costs us nothing is not a sacrifice. This is why the widow was commended by Jesus for her gift. He gave out of her lack. This is true sacrifice. He purifies our praise, fellowship and thankfulness. But he will take anything else we want to put on our altar. Our altar hearth is our heart.

When we are confident that God accepts our sacrifices, we can come boldly into His presence. We wait on His fire because we have faith to believe we have done it all as He has required of us. We wait on His deliverance. He will show up. Our face to Him in belief is the flint to the flame. The igniter is faith.

Exodus 17:15, 40.47, I Chronicles 21:26, II Chronicles 15:8, 32:12, 33:16, I Kings 18:30, Isaiah 50:7, Matthew 5:23, Acts 17.23, Hebrews 12:28-13:19.

Falling In Love

Falling, falling, falling in love with the Savior. More life, more love, more light, over and over and over. Falling and falling and falling into His fatherly sustaining arms. Lifter of my head. Maker of all things beautiful.

Tomorrow Today

Generally what happens: I pushed for tomorrow and today comes. It was a revolving door. It continues. More and more insight into tomorrow, today.

Pink Haired Girl

I gave my sweater to a girl with pink hair on a train because she needed it. I was already warm and she had goose bumps on her legs as she tried to sleep while we bumped along the track toward our mutual destination. Why do you think God gives above and beyond? So, we can give to those with pink hair. But, remember, the pink hair does not relate to their need. She was cold and did not have a mom with her to give her one. So I was her mom for a few minutes. And for a few minutes, she became my daughter. A bond born by a need met. That is how it is supposed to work. But, we let other things get in the way, things that never were meant to get in the way. Our pride, our selfishness, our apathy. Major hindrances to the growth of the Kingdom of God. God has called us to be a family. I don't really think we know what that means. Many of us never had one. So, I guess we had better ask Him about it. Because, when I lent her my sweater, it opened a way for a relationship of sharing. Then, I wrote her a poem about how Jesus loves those with pink hair, as much as those who don't. And, she was touched to the heart. So, was I. Because, even though I never knew her name, she ministered to me. For, I saw in her the face of my own daughter, who was once on drugs, on the street once. I hoped that when she was cold, someone had given her a sweater when I couldn't be there to do it.

Scrapping

What do we have when we leave the place we know we are supposed to be in? When we walk in His will, we dwell in the center. The middle, the heart. So, consequently, when we are not there, we get what is on the edges, the periphery. We get the fat that we should trim before the meat is served to others. It is not the center cut. It is scraps. If you find that you are doing a lot of fighting for your rights, think: Am I in the center, or fighting for scraps?

Checking Roots

The dream:

There is a fruit tree planted along side of several others. I grab it and pull it up to check the roots. I see that here are no big roots, only tiny ones that look like threads. They could never sustain this tree. It needs some sturdy roots to be able to withstand growing in the soil and not blowing over.

Interpretation:

If a gardener wants to check the roots on a plant, he doesn't pull it up. These fruit trees had a root system of tiny roots without any large ones. When I tugged them out of the earth, I killed them because I broke off the only roots that they had. Maybe, we question someone else's authenticity in their relationship with God. The message of the dream is that we are not to be root checkers. It is not ours. There are those with fragile roots and we have no way of knowing as we look at their foliage. We see the branches of their tree. We cannot see the roots. We damage them when we attempt to check out their root structure. It's not our job. People are fragile, be gentle.

Pray, not Prey

Only two things are carnivorous. Men and predators. Make sure that you don't fall into the second category. Don't be found stalking someone else's meetings. We are to pray for, not prey upon, one another. It doesn't really matter what religion someone is. If he believes in Jesus as God's Son who died For our sins and leads just one other person into the same, He is a hero in my book. I will say, 'Well done, Good and faithful servant. Enter Into My grace.' Theological encounters are only good If they bring us back to the gospel.

Credit

It's OK to do something and give the credit to someone else. We don't need the credit when everything we have is paid for already.

Sweet Salt

What is the difference between sugar and salt? Salt comes from the sea. It is common. It is sprinkled on nearly everything we eat. It makes us thirsty. Salt always shakes. Sometimes pinches. Just a little. Too salty is no good. Not enough salt makes the food bland. Sugar comes from cane and beets. It makes you feel special. Like kisses to one you love. It satisfies. Abundance that feeds the hunger above what is needed. It is syrup that flows from the tree of life. It is dried in the sun and air. Heated and bleached like salt. Sugar is with the dessert, not with main meal. Sugar is the voice of God. Our voice to him. Sweet communion between lovers. The sweetness the love of God. Salt is our voice of God to others. When you are sugar, you share what God is teaching you. It is sweet to you, and will make you sweet to others. Salt is a word in season. It is to be sprinkled. It comes from you seeing God. People can handle more sugar than salt. Salt is the season. Not the word. The word is from God and put in your hand. It is in season. A word in season; how sweet it is. The salt becomes sugar. Salt shouldn't be tasted. It will accent, not detract from the recipe if it's right. It needs to be the right amount, the right time, on the right food. When it's wrong, it becomes salt in the wounds of another. It is salt at the wrong time in the wrong place. Salt has lost it's flavor means that it is in the wrong season. We don't salt other's food, God does. We hand the container to the person and they shake it out. We hand ourselves over to them and God. We make ourselves available to them. Leading someone in deliverance is like salting their food. When they are a toddler, you can salt their food, but not later. Sugar is mixed in the fruit and spread on the bread. The word mixed with fruits of the Spirit. Then, you tell others how God is working in your life. If the fruit is ripe, it doesn't need much sugar. It it's green, it needs more sugar. A young Christian will need more words to tell their testimony. They will have more 'experience' in their words. An older Christian will talk about how God changed their heart. It will come with salt. It is more personal to everybody. There is incredible sweetness combined with a touch of salt. Like soy sauce, sometimes we don't notice how much salt we have eaten. They sneak in the salt to make others incredibly thirsty. And, when people get thirsty, they ask for water.

The Other side of Unusual

Go to the other side of unusual and dip your hand into the fount. Bless yourself. For it is in the name of the Father, Son and the Holy Spirit, we live, and move and have our being. And, it's in His word, not ours.

word

Lifted to Glory

He leads us to it, then, helps us walk. He helps us understand it. It's a three fold dream. We are lifted to His glory, and He is lifted to ours. We are obedient to His praise. Three fold obedience in him, He in us. He came through Jesus, then stepped back.

Severance

Severance pay is for those who don't want to quit, but the company needs to get rid of. It is compensation for work not done, but anticipated if the person stayed with the company. We can step aside from the work that God has given us at any time. He has provided a severance package ahead of time. Grace. Do you feel your department is being phased out? Maybe you need to relocate within the company. Maybe God wants to use your somewhere else. Sometimes, we are too quick to take the retirement package when all He wants to do is move us to another department. Ask the C E O.

Popcorn

The filling comes and overflows like popcorn overflows into the popper at the movie theatre. When the Holy Spirit fills us, he comes like popcorn. He comes as a seed, adds oil and salt at just the right temperature, and out comes a taste treat to be shared. Bursting goodness.

Staff of Life

If we are to be like the disciples, then we are to walk like they walked. He tells us to 'Go' Take no provisions. Only a walking stick. Take only ourselves and the staff of life. The Jesus provision. We pour out ourselves to Him. Then He pours Himself into those we minister to, as we respond to Him. It is like He becomes 'them' to us. He says that if we give a child a cup of water in His name, it is as if we have given Him a glass of water. If we have done it to the least of His children, we have done it for Him. Our goal is to be able to give to God in the presence of the other person. We close our eyes and pretend that we are putting it into the hand of God. There is a power transference that happens when we are filled with the Holy Spirit and minister to others in the presence of God. Power flows from negative to positive for the glory of God to the unity of His presence through us.

Be My Donut

Be sprinkled with My sweetness. I serve My bread with fruit, oil and sugar.

Word, and the gifts of the Holy Spirit along with My presence.

My love shared to others is the topping for the toast.

Have tea and toast in the morning.

Be the container to contain My presence My love, My Seven Spirits.

A sweet roll.

A House Repossessed

I have repossessed you. You were a ramshackle house, falling down with a crooked doorway, and cracks in the foundation. Your roof leaked. The fence had breaks in it along the back wall. The toilet wouldn't flush anymore. This house was slated for destruction. Then, you turned over the title to Me, and I repossessed you. I Took over the payments. You handed Me the book and everywhere there was red, I put you in the black. I paid all your debts. Then, I rebuilt the house, from the foundation up. I started with the rocks at the base. I cleaned out the rats and the hornets. I cleaned out the spiders and the thorns. Then, I added some girders. Some strong stuff, made of sturdy elements of grace. All the neighbors watched as I rebuilt your house. Room by room, we went over old stuff in your life. We cleaned out closets that had been shut for years.

We removed dusty thoughts of relationships. Things that needed to go away. Old food that Was stored in the kitchen was taken out and Boxed up. Then you and me had one bonfire after another. We burnt up those old pains. We torched the misery clean out of the agony of your old house. You have been healed, risen to new life, revamped. Now, I have declared an open house, for others. I don't really want to, we have invested so much time together. All that rebuilding. What wonderful time we spent on the floor Hammering away at issues, tacking up filaments of My word in the walls of your heart. And crowning you with the roof of My mercy. For, grace was the foundation and Mercy is the roof.

And, it makes Me sad to release you from the wilderness. But, I release you, today, to do My purpose. I hereby declare the open House. They can share a look as they Read the book. Your open house, built by you, remodeled by Me. My crowning glory.

My gifts flowing through You to victory. A house built for My Glory.

God Cures

Dream:

God cures the people, then carries them.

Interpretation:

God cures us like Beef Jerky. He seasons us and gives us time to soak in it. He puts us in a salt solution. The salt makes us thirsty for Him. Then, He refreshes us with the Water; the Holy Spirit, Himself. He brings us to a point; our point of need meets with His point. At those points they cross over to meet where we need healing in our lives.

Then, He keeps putting salt on us. During this stage we are not flavorful to others. Often, we are too much to be around. We act like someone who has salt in their wounds. Because we do.

God wants to open us up and pour His healing salt into our wounds. At this time in our growth, we are exposed and salty. We are not ready to be served to others. We are in the process of being cured. It is not until the time is up that we will ready. He will take those areas of hurt in our lives and bring healing from the inside out.

He is a spring that wells up from the inside. He brings his healing power from the inside just like when we eat food. We take in what He brings to us. We allow him to enter the areas that need change.

We can choose to keep our disease, and at any time reject His curing, but if we open the areas that He shows us to Him, then his healing will come. After He cures us, He heals, then He carries.

Intuitive Insubordination

When you just know He is better than you. God is better than us. His ideas are better, His plans are better, His vision is better. How come we still use our own? I don't think I have much intuitive intuition for this aspect. I keep getting in the way.

Healing Seven Ways

How do you bring healing, Lord? *The cross. Mine at yours. Meet Me at the heart. Crossover. Bring your burdens to My cross. I bring healing Mercy, grace, and forgiveness. My Cross meets at your point of need.*

The healing starts in our heart. It flows from His Holy Spirit out to His Spirit that is dwelling within us and flows through us to others. And, there is healing 7 ways. It is God's perfect number. It is His healing, not our healing.

When we go to their house instead of trying to bring them to ours, we bring God's presence to them. We bring the essence of Him. If we are in Him we bring His perfect gift. Him.

We bring the complete present because all that He is, He has given to us. He makes himself known to others through us. What I bring is perfect because I am perfect because of Him living within me. Just like perfect shoes delivered right to your door. Like glass slippers that only fit one person; like Cinderella. God will bring perfect direction, teaching, counsel, power, might.

Father, we look at others with our eyes and see what needs to be healed. I pray that You will open our spiritual eyes to enable us to see what really needs to be healed, not just what we see. Then, dear Lord, help us to follow the trail back to your power through Jesus Christ's name. Amen.

Lettuce Wraps

We are wrapped in His love and fed to others. You know? Like a lettuce wrap. Lettuce be wrapped by Him. Like a hors de vors we draw others to the table of Jesus. Let us join hands with those outside and bring them inside. That they might be rapt to Him. Moving toward getting wrapped by His love.

Fun in the Snow

The Dream:

My husband and I are in a water park. There is snow everywhere. We have fun. We go up and down the rides sliding and climbing. When we come to the end, I go out on a ledge. He calls me back to a better way. At first I am skeptical, then, I go his way.

There is a loud thunder noise. A lot of people leave the water park in a hurry, running. I didn't know they were even there because I didn't see them before. We go for a final ride down a slide. It looked like it was going to be tough but it wasn't. The snow was there to pad the way.

We go to the center to gather our stuff and they couldn't find it. Eventually we find it under a bench. It is a towel and a stethoscope without ear pieces.

Interpretation:

God has an adventure waiting for us. He wants us to have fun in our relationship with Him. When we enter into a relationship with Him that is personal, it is like going to a water park on a hot day. He brings cool refreshing water; it is enough to swim, splash and delight in. It is OK to have fun with God.

There is enough of the Holy Spirit to fill, overflow and swim in. He wants to play with us like a father plays with his children at the amusement park. He delights in us; we need to recognize it and start delighting in Him.

A lot of times, we think God is only for serious conversations. But, the message of the dream says that He wants to be for fun, too. In the dream, I am wearing my swim suit, but it is a park filled with snow. The snow symbolizes the forgiveness that Jesus offers through his blood according to Isaiah 1. 18.

We, don't need to wear clothes to His party because He has supplied them to us. We wear the robe of His righteousness through Jesus Christ.

He wants us to come in our bathing suit (actually, naked; it's a skin party) and play in His snow; to delight in His forgiveness.

He wants us to have fun with Him as our husband. He has come to release us from burdens, but we still do not let go. He has His arms extended to take our burdens and sins, but we still hang onto them. Then, they steal our delight. Only when we let go of our burdens, will be begin to delight in Him.

Sometimes, we put ourselves into a place where we do not belong. He will call us back to the place where He wants us to be. In the dream, I go out on a ledge and my husband and he calls me back to a better way. The way that he calls me to has a slide. God wants to give us His 'slide'. He has provided a slide into His way of forgiveness.

When we try to conjure up our own joy; our own fun in the 'God realm' we will not be able to do it. We find ourselves out on a limb without no firm standing. We can stand with Him, when we slip into what He has for us.

Then, in the dream, there is thunder and people leave the water park. The thunder is the word of God. When God showed up in the Old Testament on the Mountain with Moses and He spoke, the people thought it was thunder. They were frightened and ran. When God speaks to us, sometimes we become frightened and run. Why?

Maybe we are anticipating what He is going to say, and think that He will tell us that we are doomed. That is what the Children of Israel thought. They were frightened and told Moses to go forward for them and come back to tell them what God has to say. In Exodus, we can read how Moses, then ascends to the mountain and talks with God as a man talks to a man; face to face.

God wants to talk to each of us face to face, not just a select few. We need to ask Him to change the fear of Him that we have for a healthy one. If we are His children, then we can quickly claim grace and mercy, and run to His presence because we hide behind the face of Jesus when we are in His face.

Jesus stands between us and God when we are in His presence 'through Christ', so we do not have to run. If we are running from the voice of God, then there are issues that we are refusing to deal with and we are afraid that He will reveal them to us. He already knows about them. He is God and knows everything.

I have a friend who converted to Christianity from Buddhism. When she first started praying, she addressed God this way, "Dear God, This is Sarah, I am in Las Vegas (then she gave her address)."

I showed her Psalm 139 and how God knows her intimately. He knit her in the womb of her mother and continues to multiply every cell of her body up to now. Just like God knows everything about us, He also knows what we struggle with. He will be there to take it from us as we turn it over. We need to ask Him for the grace to do it.

In the dream, when we go to the center; the center of where we are supposed to be, then what we have left is not there. All of the cares that we have left at the foot of the Cross will be taken care of when we turn them over to Jesus. He only leaves a towel and a stethoscope.

The towel is for washing each other's feet. We are to enter into a ministry of serving each other as Jesus serves us.

Jesus showed the full extent of His love when He took off his outer clothing. He bared himself and wrapped Himself in what was needed to serve others. He put aside His needs and adorned Himself with what was needed to serve others needs. He poured himself out; shared His pure heart, and allowed it to become full of the dirt of the feet of the disciples.

He allowed the road dirt, the evidence of life in this sinful world to taint His cleanness. He allowed his robe of righteousness to become the cleaning rag for their feet. They were made clean by His display of a servant. We need to have a cleansed preparation for preaching the Gospel.

Our feet need to be washed by His righteousness. Our preparation for service in the Kingdom of God is in caring for the needs of those that need to be served.

Jesus brought Himself, the water of His presence, the basin (emptiness before God), openness before the men (He disrobed), and a towel. He brought the towel. He didn't just leave them wet, He brought the provision for righteousness completed.

He took away the water with His towel because He brought His presence; the Presence of God. There is no more reason for us to be thirsty because He has brought the water to us; we can be satiated. He came when we were thirsty and dirty and left us filled and clean.

Mary anointed the feet of Jesus before his burial by breaking a jar of expensive perfume and pouring it on his feet then cleansing them with her tears and wiping them with her hair. She poured out her soul to Him. She was willing to share her inner emotions and expend herself for what she knew was right and He commended her for it.

Her towel was her hair. Hair is adornment. She made only a thread between her and Jesus and cushioned it with her tears. She new truly who He was and wasn't afraid of what others thought of her. She knew He came to die for her sins and demonstrated her gratefulness to Him for His sacrifice.

She poured forth her fragrance. Her aroma filled the air. Our aroma fills whatever area that God has placed us in. We need not fear where He has placed us. Maybe there will be those who won't understand the intimacy of our relationship with Jesus, but they will respect it when they see our genuineness of heart and servant's attitude toward them.

A stethoscope is an instrument that is used by nurses and doctors for listening to our hearts to tell what kind of condition it is in. They can tell if it is functioning well. They can tell if it is sick. In the Dream, the stethoscope is without the 'ear pieces'. It is impossible for a nurse to listen to someone's heart without that piece of the stethoscope. A stethoscope is made of a bell, and two tubes that echo the noise of the sounds to two ear pieces that fit into the ears.

They enable the person to hear the heart of the one that they are listening to. In the dream there is no ear pieces. The message from God is that we are not supposed to listen to each other's hearts. It has not been given to us to know one another's' heart condition before God. This is His job, not ours. He is the one that weighs the hearts of men. He is the one that has the ability to speak directly to the heart.

We are not to assume the role of the physician in diagnosing each other's conditions. We need to leave it to the Great Physician. In fact, God says, that we are not even supposed to judge our own hearts. We are to give them into His hand and let Him judge us.

The true judge of our heart is the praise that we receive from God. When He says to us, "Well done, Good and faithful servant."

At any time we can ask God to test our hearts. He doesn't mend hearts, He makes them new. He is not interested in fixing what we have messed up. He wants to create in us a new heart. He has opened the door for us to talk to Him. It is up to us to do it.

II Chronicles 6.30, Nehemiah 13.14, Ps 7.9, 27.21, 51, Proverbs 16.2, Ecclesiastes 2.10, Isaiah 25, Jeremiah 17, Zephaniah 3, Rom 8, I Corinthians 4.5, John 12,13, Revelation 7.17, 21.4.

Reach Out

Throw the candy and the flowers to others as you ride the float down the boulevard. Reach out. Give. You didn't buy it anyway. When you are on the curb, sit as close as you can. Lean in. He doesn't ride the float and pass by. He walks the crowd, then, sits on the curb with the little ones because He wants to watch the parade, too.

Views: EKG and Mirrors

It is in the plan of God to lead the captives out from whatever is holding them from being able to be in unity with God and His plans for them.

The freedom is brought about by us using the gifts that He gives. When He trains us, He gives us gifts of the Holy Spirit and shows us how to manifest them through His Seven Spirits.

These are the faces of God. It is like looking at the heart of God using an EKG. When we take a picture of a heart with an EKG machine, it is the same heart from 12 views. It shows different sides of the same heart. God wants to show His heart to the world. He uses different views, or faces, to show it. He has given us seven 'EKG leads'. When we begin to walk into the gifting that He has given us, our life demonstrates some of those leads, or views of God to others.

We become a looking glass for others to see God through. As we look into His face, He reflects Himself onto us. Then, as we live our lives, others see His reflection from us. It is the reflection of God that we have seen as we looked into the mirror. A reflection is a 'backwards' view.

I have a necklace with the name of 'Jesus' written on it. I have a hard time putting it on so that others can read the name forward. I look into the mirror and put the necklace on so that it spells 'Jesus' to me. To others, however, the word is backwards. I have had to learn how to turn it around, so that they can read it forwards. The same way, we look into a mirror and see the 'back' of God. We cannot see His face as long as we are on earth, not in Heaven. We see the reflection of God through Jesus Christ. As we focus on Him, He reflects Himself on us.

If we start to focus on ourselves, then it is a problem when we project Him to others. Just like my necklace, they will see him spelled 'backwards' because we have put on His righteousness according to our own view of it instead of His.

We need to look at Him and not worry about what we are projecting to others. It is not our problem to project Jesus correctly, it is His. We cannot see ourselves properly. Only through His eyes do we see the correct image of ourselves.

God asks us to become humble, contrite, willing, obedient and to give Him praise. All of these elements will become natural toward someone that we have grown to love. The Holy Spirit is there to help us. We can always call on Him to give us an extra dose of grace. He promises to bear our burdens as we give them to him. Every day we can ask Him to give us salvation through the blood of Jesus. Grace provides us with victory over the enemy. We can hide in the wings of God in safety. He fights our battles for us.

The flow of God through our lives will result in Him being praised within the congregation. He will come with His voice and power to give strength to His people. He uses us to do it when we learn how to become an open valve. We learn how to lay our own desires, and let his desires for His children to flow through us. Then, He will come with power and might. We will see miracles.

Father, fill us new with Your Holy Spirit. Give us the spiritual gifts to make us what You want us to be. Help us to reflect Your image the way You want us to. Amen

Town Crier

Theologians have some pretty fancy words for ideas they did not invent. I thought men named their own inventions after themselves. Cry My Word. Be a town crier. Not one to stand in the center scream, and pound on a podium. But, to weep for My Kingdom. Let the people hear the break in your voice put there as your heart is broken because it is melted to Mine.

Angel Training

This is angel training. A ministry of grace serving others. Being there when they need you, being sent by the voice of God for a specific purpose in their life. Then, back out so God gets the glory, like an angel, because you are.

Angel Meet

We are having an angel meet. It's our meat to do His will. It is the substance that the ministry of service is made of; serving others listening to God's voice, calling on His Grace, and offering our will freely for others. That's the ministry of the cross. That is what we pick up, like a clip board when we come on duty. It tells us how to care for those God has entrusted to us. The angels have covered the night shift. They have given messages from the Father to His children, faithfully. They are our caregivers, in spirit. Yet, they have learned how to care for the needs of the Father, first. He is their God, just as He is ours, and their tribute is to Him, not us. They will do no service unless it honors His name, When we join the family of God in a ministry of service, we become like them. In that God is our Father, and we are in service to honor Him, not ourselves.

Still Meeting Angels

We bring messages to His Children, things that they need, to help encourage them and draw them closer to Him. Yet, it is only by His grace, the grace of the Dove, that we have been entrusted, and found worthy to carry the words from God. He, alone, gives us the grace, threaded through our soul like a ribbon. His ribbon of love is woven through our lives, many times in the places of brokenness,areas where we have our own needs. For, when we have called upon Him to meet our needs, then we know, for sure, He will be there to meet others' as well. But, remember, the angels are there first, ministering to those we are also sent to. It is like a hospital and we are nurses. The angel has the night shift, and we are here to come on duty now that it is day shift. They give us report on the patient, yet they don't leave. For, angels don't need to sleep. They stay to help us care for them. It takes the pressure off us, because we can go home when we need to, realizing that they will continue to be there ministering in our absence.

I Scream, Melt Down

Sometimes I feel like an ice cream sandwich on a hot day.
I melt down.
My strength drips down like melted ice cream through the fingers.
I go limp, lose drive, and give up I need hope.
So, I call out to Jesus because He says, He is the hope for us.
I cry for help.
And he is there instantly.
I never knew.
But, now I do.
It was His fingers I was melting through.

Toffee

Over and above, the sweetness overflows. The wrapped candy
overflows from the dish on the table. When we are set in the
presence of God, with the gifts He has given, we will overflow
with His sweetness. Then, He stretches us. And, sometimes, we
feel just like toffee. Toffee has a certain texture, chewy sweet flavor,
not attained by any other way. It is rolled, stretched, twisted,
and kneaded by the hand of the baker. If we feel like we have been
stretched, it is because He wants us to have a texture of His sweetness.
Then, when he gives the wrappers, we will be ready to serve others
in just the right way, He intended. When we Bring Jesus to the
Children, We bring His sweetness, covered with colorful wrapping
that He has given to us, alone. Our individual, colorful, wrapper. Our
personality, decorated with His grace. The result is like toffee. Toffee
is tender candy, that can be given to those without teeth, to chew. It
melts in our mouth, yet has a special texture.

*Tenderness abounds when His love surrounds. Bounty abounds
through hands that are willing to let go of the things that keep us from
the place He wants to take us.*

Second Hand Tunes

The Dream:

I am looking for an outfit. I am at the second hand store. I like the cartoon puzzles, but they all seem to be missing a few pieces. They might not be important, but maybe they will to others. Also, there are a lot of the same things that may not fit others that need it. I just sell what I have. It's a song. A tune to a sing, not a product.

Interpretation:

I am looking for what I am supposed to wear; my adornment. I have been at the second hand store. God says that I have been accepting second hand songs. He wants me to sing for Him myself. I am to give my own tunes to others.

I see what is missing in second hand songs. Some of them are missing essential pieces that others might need. The love and intimacy of God may not flow through like it needs to. Everyone needs to be brought closer to Him when we sing. If they aren't, then we didn't do our job.

Sing, Heart sing, your new tune. Don't go pick up a used tune. Sing with the new tune that is provided by the King of the Rock.

God's Heart Song

Above and beyond, in and through, You are my heart song, and I love you.

Second Hand Sweetness

We settle for second hand sweetness. Like nuts, we stay in our shell, thinking that somehow, by some miracle, He will get to our heart without us being willing to open up. We are insane to think we could eat the center of the filbert without opening the shell. We need to learn to submit to His hand that inflicts brokenness so that we can learn to become open to His purposes. For the Lord continues to hold in His hand, the same tool that broke our Sweet Savior.

Sugar Bowl

I found this bowl. It was full of communion with one another. I added sweetness. Sugar. I brought candy to the kids. At first,I thought they would be scared about accepting candy from a stranger. But, they were drawn to the sweetness. The bowl was a skate park in the city park and I sang Great is Thy Faithfulness to the top of my lungs sitting in a bench while they skated. I don't think any of them had gone to church, so, I brought it to them that day.

And, they brought me a new feeling of acceptance I had not known before. And for a short time, the graffiti on the cement became dim compared to the writing of God's word into their hearts. Only when I was willing to give, did they come to know the giver behind the gift.

The Rising Son

Look! Lift up your eyes. Revival is on the horizon. The Son rises again and again. Let Jesus arise in your heart and shine in those dark places. What manner of love the Father has bestowed on us that we should be called the Sons of the Most High God. He is already seated.

We don't make him rise. We just point Him out to others. Declare Him to them. Revelation has come. *I will reveal Myself to My people.*

Season Tickets

There is a tag team symphony playing. The orchestra of the Most High. Oh, that we may have season balcony box seats. The earth plays a tune of praise. No composer can compose. For the conductor Himself writes the music, builds the instruments, tunes the violins, shines the horns, brings His choir, then sits down at the drums to keep the rhythm.

Children Dancing in Puddles

The children are dancing in the puddles. The Spirit's water has overflowed in someone's life and it has gathered forming a puddle around him. And, yet, he dances. He never stopped. He didn't notice that his cup got full. Then, continued to overfill, and flow over!

But, Glory to God! When he dances, the Spirit splashes on those around bringing healing, light, deliverance, and salvation. Dance, freed soul, dance! How we love it when you overflow. For we reap blessings we never asked for.

Singing with our Heart

The dream:
I'm in a circle with many people. All are given a word; verses. I take mine to God and ask what to do with them. I end up in the midst of the others singing. Mom comes and hugs me.

Interpretation:
None of us more anointed than another. All are equal before God. He is the leader. We all encircle the throne of grace and he provides the same amount for each of us.

In the dream, I bring the word that God has given me back and ask him what to do with it. I realize that I do not know how to use the gifts that he has given me, so I ask him how the word interrelates with it. He tells me. When God tells us what to do with what he has given us, it will make us sing.

In the dream when my Mom comes and hugs me, I know that it is a representation of my trainer; mother wisdom. Psalms personifies Wisdom as our mother, our trainer. When we bring the words that God gives us back to him for clarification, he will send us Wisdom. We will be embraced by it. It will hug us.

When we step into what God has created us for, it is like a new song in our heart. When we give the words back, we take the communion and bring it into the presence with the Holy Spirit. It becomes an offering to him. His word becomes the offering. It is automatically pleasing to him because it is pure. The difference is that it has been threaded through our heart. The word has come to us,

190

through us, then back to him. When the voice of God flows through us, it causes our heart to sing. We are created to sing. Jesus talks, we sing. He is the flower, we smell. We are the fragrance.

The word, or the messages from God come to us individually. They are special to each of us.

We cannot interpret them ourselves without the help of the Holy Spirit. What happens when we bring them back to God, with the help of the Holy Spirit, is that they become alive. The breath of the Holy Spirit gets under the message and quickens the message in us. It takes on flesh. It was spirit, but by allowing the message to flow through our lips to God, it takes flesh.

It is like the 'dry bones' in Ezekiel. The prophecy is about 'dry bones'. The bones were without flesh until God gave them flesh. We are the hands of God. His messages to earth are 'dry bones' until they pass through us. They need to be given flesh to come alive. When the breath of the Lord (the Holy Spirit) passes over the Word of the Lord it comes to life and walks. God's Word walks through our life.

One I prayed the book of Revelation. That is not unusual for me. *one night* I pray books of the Bible for people all the time. This night I was praying it for a friend and her family to help rescue her son who had proclaimed he was a witch. He said that he had sold his soul to the devil. She came to me and asked for prayer. I felt led to pray the book of Revelation. I pray the words back to God. The next morning, as I was sitting on the side of my bed, I heard the voice of God.

He said, "All these things will come to pass when the breath of the Lord blows against them."

His message was clear. The book of Revelation needed to be prayed into action. I wonder how many others have?

My friend's son broke the curse of the enemy against his life, and is now going to church. The word of the Lord is stronger than any curse of the enemy. I came across someone the other day, who had made a pact with Satan. I asked him if he ever had asked Jesus to be his Savior. He responded that he had, at one time, asked Jesus to be his Savior. After I asked God about it, he told me what to say.

I went back to that young man who had sold his soul to the devil and I told him to just tell the Devil that the deal is off. After all, Jesus is in charge, and he had given his soul to Him first. The Devil was tricking him into believing that he owned him, when in fact, he was a child of God. He did, and was healed of his drug addiction.

When we have a dream or a vision and we bring it back to God and ask him to interpret it for us, then we are bringing his word back to him. Then, when he interprets it, we can act on it. As we act on it, it is like the dry bones coming to life. The Word has been given life through us.

Each of us is special. God gives us our own messages. They are like tunes into our heart. When we bring them to him and ask him to help us with interpreting them, he gives us the instruments to play the tune that he wants us to play in the orchestra of his Church.

It is a new song that has never been sang by anyone. It is a heart song. We can't learn it from someone else because it has never been sung before. It is new. When we stand next to some one with a singing heart, we can feel it. They don't need to say anything. We know. Our spirit bears witness to their spirit that it is the Spirit of God that is making them sing. When we sing with Jesus, we don't need to tell anyone. They will know.

The Angels shout for joy because the temple of God is being built. We are His Holy temple. He makes His dwelling within us by the Holy Spirit. We are the stones which He builds his Kingdom of. Each time we bring His Words back to Him for interpretation, a new stone is cut.

It is the key He has put in our hands that opens the door for others to enrich the Kingdom of God. As we sing, the Lord will fulfill his purposes for us. The angels lean forward to hear us to catch the key. These notes have never before been played. When we sing the song that He has put in our hearts, we will do the gift that He has called us to do.

As we step out with the song he has put in our heart and sing it whole heartedly, he will trust us with his plans. He will start to reveal more and more of his desires to us .

Those who have learned how to walk in their gifting, will recognize Him when He shows up.

They will be the first to see Him. Their job is to announce His arrival to others. They are to tell the children to 'pay attention, God is here!"

God sings, too. His heart is stirred when we see something that He is trying to show us. He shouts over us with singing. He is thrilled when our paths are lit and we do not walk in darkness anymore.

When His voice is interpreted to us, this brings direction to us. He loves to guide us with His song. It is His song responding to our song. Song to song, in response to our service.

We praise Him with our songs. There is no need to worry about us drowning Him out with our singing. We cannot sing over His voice. I am sure that our voice is a squeak compared to His. As we put Him in control of the relationship, He will quiet our singing when He wants to sing to us. He stills our heart, when He wants to talk to us. He simply overwhelms us. He quiets us with His love. He kisses us.

Job 38, Psalms 30, 66, 100, 138, Isaiah 5, 35.6, 42, 52, 54, Ezekiel 37, Zephaniah 3, Rom 10, I Corinthians 14, Ephesians 5, Colossians 3, Hebrews 2, Revelation 5.9, 14.

Late Praise

God is enthralled with our praise when we provide a place for him to sit and we elevate Him, put His name above ours.

We are the only voice in the world.

If we do not speak, then there is no praise of God.

There is song.

For surely the birds sing to Him.

There is peeping cheeping and roaring.

There is raising of paws and boughs of trees.

There is laud in the movement of the brook down the ravine over the falls. The noise praises Him.

But, only man has been given the capacity to form words, tell others, and perform deeds that bring laud to Our Savior.

Do you wonder?

Do you lack belief?

go Do out your door and sing a song of praise.

Then listen. Sing again. Then listen.

See if the birds don't join.

They will.

For, they were already singing of His praise and they are delighted to have you join in.

They started a long time ago.

You are the one who is late.

Love Signs the Picture

The Dream:

My husband and I go out to eat at a dinner all the time. We are regulars. Paul would often serve us as we dined there. He was known by all the workers, as one of them.

One day we went with a group where there was a special dinner. The servers were rude to Paul because they thought he had crashed the party and didn't belong there with the elite. Because they already knew him, it was hard for them to picture it in their mind as him being someone special.

Word: *Awesome love signs the picture.*

Interpretation:

The husband in the dream represents Jesus, as my husband. Jesus is to become the husband of the Church and the Church is to be his bride. Also, in the Old Testament, God describes himself as a husband, one like a gardener, who trims bushes. He wants to have a relationship like a husband, both way, with us. He wants to tend us, like a gardener, and He also wants to be our close companion, like a husband.

Often, in dreams, God uses the closest 'like' model that He can find. For me, He uses my husband to represent my relationship with him.

In the dream, my husband and I go to a restaurant that we frequent, except this time he comes as a guest instead of a regular. He was always a guest, but in the mind of those who worked there, He was like one of them because He did not put a separation between them and Himself. He did not look down on them as the ones who should serve Him.

So, when the time came for them to do their job, they didn't come through. They became indignant at Him without cause. He merely came back to claim the position that He always had, but had not claimed until now. They assumed, because He acted like a servant, that they did not owe Him respect, but they were wrong.

There are similarities with Jesus within the dream. In our relationship with Him, we can see that He came as a servant, serving us, at first. He was God, yet, He did not claim any of the honor that was due to His name. Rather, He put aside His honor, and acted like one of the servers in a restaurant would, serving His own coffee along side of them.

So, when He returns to us, will we honor Him the way He should be? He was always God, yet, He was not honored as God while he lived his life on the earth for thirty-some years.

Our relationship with God is personal, yet we must realize that He is still God, and we are the ones who are people. He deserves our honor, even though He does not demand it.

It is because of his special type of love, that He is OK to have a position, yet not claim it. Do we? Just because have been given a position, does not mean that we have to tout it. We need to follow His example.

For, it is His awesome love that signs His picture. Jesus is a picture of the love of God given to us. By His love, He came to earth, gave up His rights as God, and demonstrated how to serve. He is our example of how we should serve others.

Father, help us to follow the example of Jesus, not claiming our own position, but being willing to set it aside for others. Help us understand what it means to be a servant.

Testimonial Music

Picture albums show photographs of history to help us remember times from the past. We keep them in a place where we can open them to recall events over and over as often as we desire. Record albums are impressions into vinyl of songs we have grown to love. We keep them in a place to play them over as we desire. Why? There is a joy that comes to our soul when we recall fond memories, and sing familiar tunes with ones we care about. Both albums are meant to be shared then and now. God's visions are His photo albums of our lives. We need to record the visions and show the growth of the vision into maturation for our loved ones to see. Just like a baby, a vision is given To us. It grows into ministry. Record it and play it over and over for others. That is called testimony. Music to God's ears. For, it's the freedom march to lead others to making albums of their own.

Billow My Sail

Billow my sail, sweet voice of Jesus.
Blow through my life, cease me from strife.
In thee do I hope, I hand you the rope.
Take the wheel, dear Lord.
Billow my sail.

Comfort my soul, come make me whole.
In thee do I trust.
I love you, I love you, you must
Billow my sail.

Air my desires, stop Satan's conspires.
My life is in your hands, dear Lord.
Complete all your plans.
Bring air to my breath, your sweetness to my being.
Lover of my soul, bring me to the path of seeing.

Billow my sail, Dear Jesus.
How I love you, and it's useless
To hope in another, for no other,
None, can love me like my Mother,
My Father, and my Friend, and my Lover.
Sweet Jesus

Writing Index

About the Author

Sheri Hauser grew up in Seattle, Washington accustomed to the rainy days and nights going on long hikes in the Cascades in the summer and snow skiing in the winter. She graduated from High School in Leavenworth, Washington and attended Bible College in Oregon. Married at 20, she went on to nursing school and had two children. In 2001, she began writing spiritual books and started to look for a publisher. Not finding one who would accept her manuscript, she opted to learn what was needed to grow her own publishing company. Initially the company was called Glory Bound Books and obtained license in Las Vegas in 2005. As the company grew, she tossed her entire nursing paycheck into purchasing printers and software. She attended classes at the University of Las Vegas for graphic design, web site development and photo shop. It took three years of intensive study to learn papers, the publishing industry and how to put books together. Throughout this time, she developed the Lasertrain (a set of digital templates for making your own books). She climbed the ladder of her profession and after 30 years as a Cardiothoracic Nurse in Intensive Care, she retired from nursing full-time to dedicate her time to grow a publishing company. By 2016, she had written 25 books, and published over 600 books (from authors).

Her and her husband relocated to Camp Verde, Arizona in 2017 and set the publishing company in an old house living in the upstairs. They love the quiet cowboy town and she is presently active in forming a newly developing Chamber of

Commerce. She is the president.

Additionally, she is part of the Curriculum Development Team and a Facilitator teaching classes related to publishing at Osher Life Long Learning Institute in Sedona, Clarkdale and Camp Verde.

2020 started off with a bang when she began doing ads on Amazon for her books. Today, she has 15 books on page 1 of their topic search engines and is actively seeing sales daily.

Sheri Hauser is the author of several series of books including: Glorybound Lasertrain, Dream Books with Steps to Intimacy with God, GBK Children's books and text books on publishing.

Glorybound Publishing

dream
books

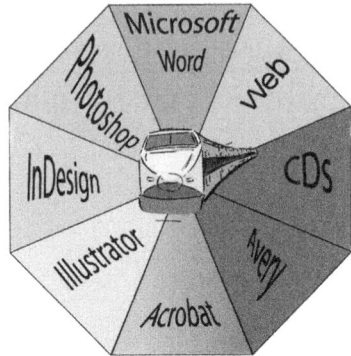

Microsoft Word
Photoshop
Web
InDesign
CDS
Illustrator
Avery
Acrobat

GLORYBOUND LASERTRAIN

GBK™

Sheri's Books

The manuals are books which help prepare for the release of the prophetic wave of the Holy Spirit as spoken of in Joel 2. These books are written from dreams. The dreams were given over a period of around 6 months or so. As they were received, I carefully interpreted them using Scriptures. Then I was given an outline dream. The dreams of the specific subject were then put into the outline. That forms the books. There are 21 books. Initially, all of the books were as one giant book. Then as I received more dreams of direction, the books began to split; first into four, then into more (like bread rising in a bowl) they grew over time within the right environment. The first book split into what became the first four books. I was instructed to turn over the stack and release them. So, I released Coriantá, having it professionally edited and printed at the cost of $37,000. By the time I got to the next book, I realized that the books were reproducing at an alarming rate, and I would never have enough money to print them conventionally, so I asked God if I could have a publishing company.

He said, "Sure."

I quickly responded, "I don't know anything about a publishing company."

His response, "That's OK. It will come in a box with instructions."

I quickly called the guy who put together my first book and then ordered the computer program which he specified as the one for making books. Guess what? It came in a box with instructions. (Smile). Several of the books sprouted due to the response from individuals asking questions--such as *Simple Fun Christian Dream Interpretation*, the three books in the Prophetic Prayer Series as well as *Prophetic Interpretation of Art*.

All of the books are available as e-books and bound copies regular and large print through Amazon.com. Printed bound, signed, color editions are available directly through Glorybound Publishing. Use the contact page on the web site to order.

The Prophetic Wave

Manuals for a Prophetic Wave of the Holy Spirit with Miracles, Signs and Wonders

And Afterwards I will Pour Out My Spirit
Christian Authors Driving the Market
Dream Language Understood
Faith on a Wing and a Prayer
Filled with the Holy Spirit
Foundational Prophetic Prayer
Going to the Center of God's Heart
Growing Ministry to Seed instead of Fruit
Inspirational 3-D Poetry
Intimate Relationship with Jesus
Leading Prophetic Prayer
Living in the Haunted House of my Head
Living in the Shadow of the Sins of our Parents
Personal Prophetic Prayer
Preparing the Bride of Christ: Allegorical
Prophetic Interpretation of Art
Sharing Prophetic Gifts in the Church
Simple Fun Christian Dream Interpretation
Spiritual Authority Over Demon Dragons
Tactical Demonic Warfare
Why the Glory Departed

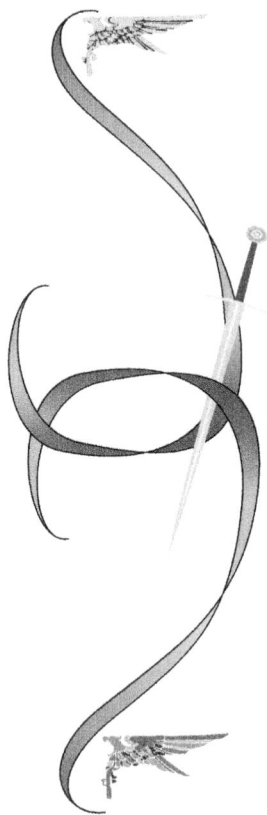

Made in the USA
Monee, IL
25 January 2021